D0681365

Literary Agents

Literary Agents

A WRITER'S INTRODUCTION

Featuring In-Depth Interviews with
the People Who Make It Happen

BY JOHN F. BAKER

Macmillan • USA

MACMILLAN
A Pearson Education Macmillan Company
1633 Broadway
New York, NY 10019-6785

Library of Congress Cataloging-in-Publication Data
Baker, John F., 1931–
        Literary agents : a writer's introduction / by John F. Baker
        p. cm.
Includes index.
ISBN 0-02-861740-1 (alk. paper)
        1. Literary agents—Interviews
                I. Title
PN163.B35   1999
070.5'2—dc21 98-50769 CIP

Printed in the United States of America
10 9 8 7 6 5 4 3 2

Book design by George McKeon

Contents

v

Contents

Introduction

Literary agents are the uncrowned queens and kings of the book publishing business today. Publishers and editors, who have traditionally held that hallowed position, may strenuously object, but there seems little doubt that it is the agents who, often for better and occasionally for worse, have shaped the current literary landscape. It is true that they have been partly responsible for much too much money often being paid for transparently unworthy books (though publisher insecurity and cupidity have been at least as much to blame); but is also true that in recent years it is the agents, rather than the editors and publishers, who have discovered most of the significant new talent, nurtured the authors, often helped shape their work to best effect, and guided their careers. It may be a commonplace to note that the agent these days is usually the only fixed element in an author's life, since many publishers and editors have become equivocal and migratory, respectively; the one shying away from any sign of falling sales, the other ever on the lookout for a better salary at another house; but it is largely true.

As a result of their growing significance as arbiters and gatekeepers, then, agents have in effect supplanted the roles once played by the legendary figures (Alfred Knopf as publisher, Maxwell Perkins as editor) who dance in every author's or would-be author's head. The most desperate search among the countless aspiring writers today is no longer for the ideal publisher, but for the perfect and all-powerful agent—the assumption being that once the right agent has taken you in hand, the longed-for publication experience will surely follow. It is on the agent's table that the urgent letters, the fervent proposals, the tottering manuscripts pile up these days rather than the publisher's. The savvier would-be authors have long ago concluded that publishers will not read them, whereas an agent, especially a comparatively new one eager for new clients, just might. It is certainly a fact that many publishers will not seriously consider an unagented submission (though most still have someone glance at the so-called "slush," as such submissions are called, on the sly, just in case lightning may strike). It is also true that having a reputable agent greatly increases the chance of a foot in the door for the would-be author.

But it is something of a Catch-22 situation. Although there are now more agents than ever before—approximately 550 are listed in the current Literary Marketplace, and even more can be found in some other, less rigorous compilations—so many of them now find their client lists so crowded, and the efforts needed to sell new authors so daunting, that they take on such people only rarely. The would-be author therefore has to persuade an appropriate agent that he or she is a publishable entity as the first step on the arduous road toward publication; but at least, having succeeded in this first difficult step, they have what is presumed to be an effective, efficient and well-connected advocate on their side, and can safely leave the biggest battles of all to them.

The Role of the Agent

Just what do agents do? Their task is simple in essence: to act as the author's representative in all dealings with a publisher. This involves, first, deciding what editors at what publishing houses would most likely be interested in a book, and sending it to them, either one at a time or, more commonly, in groups (multiple submission); when it is accepted, securing the best possible payment for the book, usually in the form of an advance against royalties that will be paid out in stages; monitoring the contract the author signs with the publisher to ensure that it is fair and equitable; after a book is sold to a publisher, tracking it through the various publication stages and ensuring that the publisher is doing everything the contract promised in the way of editing, support, design and consultation; pursuing, checking and transmitting later royalty payments, if any; and deciding where, and to whom, various subsidiary rights in the book may be sold, including paperback, book club, newspaper or magazine serialization, overseas translation rights, book or movie options, even, these days, electronic rights. (Sometimes the publisher will pay extra to obtain some or all of these rights, and do such further selling themselves; the experienced agent with good international and Hollywood connections—and most have developed them—will prefer to retain such rights, feeling that he or she can sell them more effectively.)

These are the tangible services the agent performs. Increasingly these days, however, a great deal of time and effort is spent on the intangibles. Now that editors are for the most part much less nurturing of their writers, publishers less inclined to take on an author for the long haul, the agent is expected to be a combination of editor, psychologist and confessor, constantly available for consultation, advice, commiseration and congratulation. Once editors enjoyed that kind of close relationship with their authors, and a handful still do; but most editors are seen these days as at best fair-weather friends, whose loyalties are perforce at least as much to the company that employs them as to the authors they publish. The agent's sole loyalty is to the author.

What Agents Get Paid

In recompense for all these services, the agent normally receives a 15% commission on the author's earnings from the books the agent represents (not necessarily from other work, like journalism, the author may do, unless it is so spelled out). Foreign sales, because they are more irksome and time-consuming, are usually commissioned at 20%. Agents will usually absorb normal costs of doing business, though their approaches vary as to what they regard as normal: some charge for all photocopying of manuscripts, others only for excessive amounts. There is similar variability in terms of phone and postage costs. Agents are not expected to charge for the often considerable time they spend on reading unsolicited submissions, making editorial suggestions for the improvement of the manuscript, doctoring the book proposal to the point of irresistibility, finding collaborators as needed, and the many other tasks that precede a sale. Those that do charge for such services are known as fee readers, and are frowned upon by many of their less permissive colleagues, who do not allow such people to join the professional agents' body, the Association of Authors' Representatives.

The AAR, to which a large number of agents belong, has a code of professional ethics, and only accepts members who have conducted a specified number of legitimate book deals with publishers, so membership, which is noted in the capsule listings in this book, is a guarantee of a level of professionalism, experience and ethical conduct. Lack of membership, however, need not necessarily be interpreted as a sign of amateurism, malfeasance or deviousness; some people are simply not joiners, or may have specific reasons for not belonging. (One agent we know objects to the AAR because, though they no longer allow fee reading, they refused to expel members who had done so while it was still permitted.)

Agents, as the following pages will show, come from all sorts of backgrounds, but most of them started out with the same kinds of urges and ambitions that take people into book publishing in the first place: a love of good writing, a passion for reading, an inclination to spend a life associated with books and their creators. Many of them were once editors themselves, or performed other publishing functions: marketing, publicity, sales.

A few are, or were, actually published writers, and therefore especially aware of the many insecurities in a writer's life. Almost all, however, have a disdain for organized corporate life, an entrepreneurial drive, and a determination to succeed on their own that takes them through the tough times that marked the start-up years of most of today's successful agents.

Why the Agents in This Book?

The interviews that appear in this book were conducted for the most part during late 1997 and the first half of 1998, a frame of reference that should be taken into account when current or immediate past successes are discussed, as they often are. The agents were chosen as a fairly representative cross-section of independent practitioners—meaning, essentially, comparatively small-scaled, often family-owned enterprises. Agents at the larger agencies, like William Morris, ICM and Curtis Brown were not included, not because they do not have superb clients and play a very significant role in the book world, but because they are essentially employees rather than individual entrepreneurs— and also because, from the point of view of the aspiring writers who may be the keenest readers of this book, they are even less likely than the smaller, independent agents to have room on their lists for newcomers. Hence the omission of notable agents nearly every aspiring writer has heard of, such as Amanda Urban and Esther Newberg at ICM, Andrew Wylie, Robert Gottlieb of William Morris, and the all-powerful Morton Janklow and Lynn Nesbit of their eponymous firm. A handful of agents we might have wished to include chose, for whatever reasons, not to be interviewed for the book, though most of those approached agreed gladly to talk about their work. Every attempt was made to make those included a representative sample, in terms of their styles and ranges of interest, from ultra-commercial practitioners to those maintaining a mostly literary list, from people who favor fiction to those who set out to create salable books from newspaper headlines and willing journalists.

A word on geography: There is a tendency among beginning writers to believe that New York agents only deal with people they regularly see, and that their outlook is therefore circumscribed by their location. In fact the majority of most agents' clients live outside New York (it's an expensive place to live for a writer), and get to see their agents quite seldom in the flesh; some never meet at all, and conduct all their business by phone, fax, and e-mail. Writers can, and do, live everywhere, and there is an impression among agents that there are probably more writers, or would-be writers, per head of the population in California than anywhere else in the country. The majority of the biggest and most powerful agencies are in New York, true, and many of the best independents; but there has been a huge growth in the numbers who now practice elsewhere, particularly on the West Coast, and a handful of notable agents outside New York have been included here.

The aim in all the interviews has been to give readers—including, presumably, many aspiring writers—an insight into the agent's life: how he or she began, their backgrounds and special interests, their early clients, how their lists developed, the kinds of books and authors they look for, and how they deal, on a day-to-day basis, with the publishing climate of today—along with a sense of how that climate has changed within the working lifetimes of most of them. Agents, unlike authors or even editors and publishers, are seldom interviewed, and much of the material in this book is therefore unique. It is to be hoped that it will give its readers a much better idea than they have ever had before of how these most important players in the book world think and operate—and, in the process, a better sense of who might or not be receptive to their work. All of the agents who are interviewed here are thoroughly well established, many of them for 30 years or more, no one for fewer than five; all are well respected by editors and by their peers. Accompanying each interview is a box listing the essentials of the agent in question: address and phone and fax numbers, a sketch of the balance of the list, specialties, if any, some of the more celebrated clients, and a respresentative quote from the subject. At the end of the book is a brief listing of some other agents who have a reputation of being responsive and helpful to would-be authors, and who have a good reputation among their peers. It must be stressed again, however, that the 70 or so agents interviewed and listed in this book are only a representative sample, by no means exhaustive, of the hundreds who are active today, and who can be found listed in such publications, available in any public library, as Bowker's *Literary Marketplace*.

How to Approach an Agent

Each of the agents interviewed here was asked how best aspiring writers could approach them. Their answers were so universally similar that they are condensed here, so as not to clutter up the text, or the fact boxes, with unnecessary repetition. Almost invariably, with only a handful of exceptions as noted, agents do not welcome—and some will not even accept—phone queries. Not all those with e-mail addresses welcome e-mail inquiries. The preferred form of approach is by an initial letter which sets out as invitingly and concisely as possible the nature of the book. If it is a fiction work, there should be a synopsis and an indication of what kind of book it is: mainstream contemporary, historical, literary, genre of some kind (mystery, horror, romance). For nonfiction there should be a brief account of the ground the book will cover, a listing of the author's qualifications for writing it, a sense of what else is out there on similar subjects or with a similar approach, and something about the marketing skills and built-in readership (if any) the author can bring to the project.

Remember that the writing in such letters and proposals should be every bit as effective as the writing in the book itself. The letter is the medium by which the agent will initially assess your abilities as a writer, and if the writing is trite and cliché-ridden, the spelling or grammar less than ideal, the claims for likely readership overblown or patently unrealistic, the answer will be no. Several agents interviewed in this book say how much easier it is for editors to say no than yes; the same applies to them. Agents are longing to find really striking new clients, and the fact that they keep checking on their unsolicited submissions to make sure they are not missing anything shows how eternally that hope flickers. For almost any agent, a letter that astonishes with the brilliance or acuity of its writing, the uniqueness of its voice, the authority or knowledgability with which it treats its subject, will inspire sufficient interest for a follow-up, no matter how world-weary some of them may sound in their interviews.

If the original query letter has inspired interest, the agent will normally ask to see more. In the case of fiction they will usually ask to see the whole manuscript (and a contract with a new writer will hardly ever be signed without a reading of that full manuscript); they may wish to form a judgment, in order to save their time, on the basis of only two or three chapters—and some claim they can tell within the first few pages if something is going to work or not. In the case of a nonfiction work, they do not expect to see a full manuscript. They will ask for a formal proposal, something that can be submitted to a publisher, outlining the book's contents, probable length, needed illustrations (if any) and an estimate of the expected time needed to complete it; once again, a few sample chapters, probably including an introduction or foreword, will be required. The marketing side of any successful proposal is increasingly important, as you will see from the interviews that follow: what are the author's special qualifications? (And anything, like a popular newspaper or magazine column, a regular TV or radio show, or identification with some successful business like a health or beauty studio, restaurant or hairdresser, that can guarantee a built-in readership, will help enormously.) To what kind of readership could the book be sold? How is it different from other available books that cover similar ground? How could it be promoted and marketed, and to what audiences? What public relations skills does the author offer? Because the nonfiction proposal is all-important (an editor is, after all, deciding on the basis of the proposal, not the finished book), you can expect an agent to work closely with you on getting it just right.

It is axiomatic, by the way, that any unsolicited materials, even if only in the form of a brief query letter, must have return postage, usually a stamped, self-addressed envelope, included. Agents are not going to spend their own money mailing back unwanted manuscripts or bulky proposals, or even on stamps for proforma rejection letters.

A Highly Personal Link

Ultimately, the agent-author link is an extremely personal one, and a successful relationship is going to depend to a remarkable degree on human chemistry. The real significance of this book to a writer or would-be writer is that it suggests, in these brief portrait sketches of the agents and their work, the kinds of personalities and interests, as represented in their clients and their attitudes, to which a writer might best respond. Whether or not it helps any writer find the perfect agent for them, however, the book is still an extremely up-to-date picture of the current potentialities—and pitfalls—of the publishing marketplace.

Dominick Abel
Dominick Abel Literary Agency, Inc.

The first thing that strikes the eye in the small Upper West Side ground-floor apartment that serves Dominick Abel as his office is the shelves—lined not with clients' books (they're in a back room), but with a world-class collection of colorful clay works from a long-defunct pottery in Zanesville, Ohio. Abel and his wife have been gathering this material, once sold for dimes in dime stores but now highly collectible, for years, and he gazes at it fondly as he describes his trips to out-of-the way Midwestern country auctions where you can still occasionally pick up some good pieces.

It seems somehow appropriate that Abel, whose list consists largely of mystery and suspense writers ("That's most of what I do") should have the kind of offbeat hobby that could easily turn up in a detective story. A tall, graying man with a rather scholarly air and an English accent that reflects an early colonial and United Kingdom–based life, Abel actually began as an agent in Chicago after a brief career as a magazine and later a book editor. He was born in India, educated in Britain, became a schoolteacher in Uganda for a time, then came to the United States expecting to do postgraduate work in African studies at Northwestern. Finding he cordially disliked it, he quit in his first term, got an editorial job at a magazine called *Christian Century*, thence to the Henry Regnery publishing company, located in Chicago (and now no relation to the right-wing company run by Alfred Regnery).

He was there for seven years before he decided that when it came to choosing between publisher and author, his sympathies were on the side of the latter. "You're sympathetic to the author, but you're paid by the publisher, and you can only say no to an author as long as you're comfortable with that decision. When you're not, it becomes a problem. I found I wanted to be answerable to authors alone, to be a constant in their life; and in fact I have clients I've had forever. Stuart Kaminsky was one of my first and he's still with me; though he's been through many editors and publishers, he's had only one agent, and I find that extremely satisfying. Very few editors can say they've worked with the same author for twenty years or more."

"I found I wanted to be answerable to authors alone, to be a constant in their lives."

His sympathies being what they were, agenting seemed a natural career for him. In any event, "It was a case of Hobson's choice," he says, using an old English phrase for a decision where there is no real choice. "I was very lucky to be starting up when and where I did." Chicago in 1975 had more publishing houses than now, but no real agent, at a time when writers were beginning to realize they needed one. "Publishing was bigger then, in the sense of more markets, and many writers didn't have agents. And a Chicago agent seemed a bit exotic to New York editors. They were very generous with their time whenever I went to New York: I'd have breakfasts, lunches, dinners lined up. They probably gave me more time than they would to the local agents they were used to."

Two years later his wife, who was book editor at the *Chicago Tribune*, got a job as executive editor of the Literary Guild, and since both had always wanted to live in New York, they made the move. He built his clientele in the usual way. "I made a lot of calls, got a lot of referrals, went to writers' conferences for the first ten years or so." These he found less useful for the writer contacts than for the chance to enlarge his acquaintance among editors and other agents. "It's also useful to help give you a view beyond the Hudson. We're somewhat parochial in New York, and seeing how differently people think and work 'out there' is like a cold shower, it's good for you."

He probably has, he says, seventy-five to eighty active clients, though he quibbles a bit about what is meant by "active": "One of my writers has done only two books in ten years, whereas another writes two or three a year, but I regard them both as active." In any case, his fiction list contains some fifty names, which makes his percentage estimate of 75-25 in favor of fiction about right. His authors include a number of Edgar winners and such trailblazers among women mystery writers as Sharyn McCrumb, Sara Paretsky, Susan Dunlap, and Joan Hess; Loren Estleman, John Lutz, Bill Pronzini, and Barbara Michaels are also in his stable. He has no particular nonfiction specialties, though he doesn't do what he calls historic biography (recent subjects for Abel biographers include Jerzy Kosinski and Clark Clifford) or history, tending to contemporary subjects like self-help, parenting, the occasional specialty cookbook, management, and business.

But mystery is where his heart is (a mystery he defines as a book that has a sleuth, either amateur or professional, who usually gets paid for the work) and it is a market, particularly for series heroes or heroines, that he finds still very healthy, "though the window of opportunity closes more quickly these days." By this he means that publishers are more impatient to see a series pay off. "They're not so likely to stay with an author for the long haul; they'd rather sign up a previously unpublished author. I know lots of authors who've done fifteen or twenty books in a series, and you won't see many of those in future. Yes, it's true that good authors are finding it harder to get published, and I think it's very short-sighted. If they're good, why throw them out?"

He goes on vigorously, in carefully formulated sentences: "I understand the demand for sales, we all want that. 'We only want big books.' So do we all, but it's not so simple. The junking of quality writers in favor of writers who may not have what it takes means the same process will just be repeated, again and again." He shares the common complaint of slow contracts and payments: "There've always been people who were slow, but now there are very few who are quick." And he mentions an author doing a "quickie" book in about six weeks, which will be finished before he has even received a contract for it. There seem, he thinks, to be fewer people nowadays in each of the publishers' departments that work with authors.

He also perceives a significant gap among editors. "Today there are a number of senior people and a lot of very junior people. There were a lot of firings a few years ago when publishers took out the whole middle level, and it's never come back. So there's probably much less on-the-job training than there used to be, and younger editors can't learn as much as their predecessors did. Publishing houses are much less respectful of editors' opinions now, they're easily second-guessed by sales and marketing people. But that leads to irresponsibility—they can always blame someone else. Editors should be given more authority. They were hired to exercise their judgment, make decisions. If everyone else can now make the decisions editors were hired to make, why have them at all? They think it can all be done by numbers, but it can't; choosing a book to publish doesn't lend itself to template, formulaic procedures, and to pretend otherwise is to ignore reality."

So the need for agents, as he sees it, is greater than ever. "When so many editors now are simply acquisitions people, who don't do line-editing and leave that to freelance people who may or may not be any good, the author is essentially left to his own devices, i.e., the agent."

All this means Abel feels he is "having a good time, but that's not the same as being completely satisfied. I want more for my authors, no matter how successful. I want them to be better appreciated." As for the flow of unsolicited material, "I think writers have finally got that straight, so we get lots of queries but very few actual manuscripts any more." He and his assistant read them all, "and many are so clearly not for us that it's not too much of a burden. It's the very few that just may be for us, that's the problem. Should we or shouldn't we?"

WHO: Dominick Abel Literary Agency, Inc.

WHERE: 146 West 82nd St. (Ste. 1B)
New York, NY 10024
212-877-0710; fax: 212-595-3133

WHAT: Adult fiction and nonfiction, specializing in mystery and suspense.

LIST: About fifty-five clients, approximately 75 percent fiction. Clients include: Susan Dunlap, Loren Estleman, Stuart Kaminsky, John Lutz, Sharyn McCrumb, Sara Paretsky, Barbara Michaels, Bill Pronzini, Paco I. Taibo II, Susan Wolfe.

Member of AAR

Virginia Barber

Virginia Barber Literary Agency, Inc.

Virginia Barber, familiarly known as Ginger, runs Virginia Barber Associates out of a top-floor suite of offices on lower Fifth Avenue. She is a pretty, lively, petite woman whose voice still bears traces of her native South—and who admits that when she is trolling on behalf of a Southern client, like bestselling novelist Anne Rivers Siddons, for example, the voice slows down from its usual rapid-fire enthusiasm to become much more honeyed and measured.

Rather unusually among agents, she came to the profession from the world of academe. After getting her Ph.D. at Duke (her thesis was on poet William Carlos Williams), she became an assistant professor at Teachers College at Columbia University, offering what was called "Critical Perspectives" in British and American literature. "Actually, I was teaching things I wanted to learn about myself," she says with a laugh. She might have stayed in that world, in fact, had it not been for a bitter university dispute over tenure for a long-serving woman professor. At that time, at the beginning of the 1970s, there were no tenured female professors at Columbia, and Barber was deeply demoralized and disillusioned over the way the issue was handled by the university.

Theatrical agent Helen Merrill was a friend, and the pair decided to go into business together as agents, Merrill continuing to handle theatrical clients, Barber taking on literary ones. "I had some of the right abilities," she recalls. "I knew how to evaluate manuscripts, but not how to find the authors of them." She searched eagerly, writing to authors of stories she liked to see if they wanted to do a book, but didn't know enough back then to attend writers' conferences. "You had to be invited, and nobody knew I existed. And I was very shy and diffident."

One of the authors she took on in those early years was Rosellen Brown, who has stayed with Barber for thirty years, finally achieving bestsellerdom only four years ago with *Before and After,* which later became an admired movie with Meryl Streep. For many years Brown was published by Robert Gottlieb at Knopf and received excellent reviews, but unspectacular sales, for a series of novels that included *Civil Wars* and *Tender Mercies.* Then Gottlieb left to edit the *New Yorker,* and Barber decided it was time to switch publishers. She sent *Before and After* to John Glusman at Farrar, Straus & Giroux. "He did a terrific job, got it out to the scouts, there was an early movie sale, then a lot of foreign rights sales." Paperback rights eventually went to Dell, for a hefty six-figure sum.

But all of this was way ahead for the struggling young agent in 1972, who found that after a couple of years together she and Merrill were too different in their personalities and interests to make a go of it, and decided to split up. Two agent friends kept Barber going at this time, Elaine Markson and Phoebe Larmore, who shared offices and sent occasional clients her way. One was a man who wrote books for movie professionals. "He wrote six of them, and I still get royalties." Another was Alice Munro, the celebrated Canadian writer, who like many Canadians at that time ("I got a lot of them") was unrepresented. Larmore urged Barber to write Munro and offer her services, but at first Munro said she didn't feel she needed an agent. When Barber persisted, sending her an early Rosellen Brown book as an example of a client's work, "Alice wrote back saying any agent who represents a writer as good as that is okay by me," and another long relationship was born.

For a time Barber had a tiny office in the Flatiron Building, until one day when the phones went out. "That nearly put me out of business, because an agent can't function without a phone." Markson and Larmore then asked her to join them in their little Greenwich Village office suite. They shared a receptionist, and things were cozy for a while until Larmore went off to Los Angeles, where she still practices, and Barber took over her space. She stayed eight years, but her list kept growing and "after a while we had people hanging from the rafters," so she opened an office in the Chelsea brownstone where she lives with her husband Edwin Barber, then editorial director at W.W. Norton, now an editorial consultant for that house.

A marriage between an agent and a publishing executive is a comparatively unusual circumstance, and Ginger found it had distinct advantages and disadvantages. "You can go over manuscripts together and get a professional second opinion right at home. And of course you both understand when you each bury your head in a manuscript after supper." But their views on many questions are, inevitably, diametrically opposed. "We spontaneously think differently as publisher and agent. And of course I could never, never, deal directly with him on a book." In fact Edwin had a rule that he would never be told about submissions she had made to Norton, and would never discuss them. This naturally had a somewhat dampening effect on submitting books to that house.

One of the subjects on which would differ most strongly was on publishers' payment policies. "They'll go through any contortion to try and avoid having to pay you as soon as they should," she fulminates. "They'll say the only man who can sign the checks is out sick, or on holiday. I always feel like asking how do *they* manage to get paid then? They practice this built-in lateness, of course, because they want to keep the money in the bank earning interest. Meanwhile, authors have families, and they need the money, often a lot more urgently than the publishers do. I don't need it so much myself any more, but I still identify strongly with the poor author."

Her academic training helped Barber in one important way. She became a keen student of various publishers' author contracts, studying them one by one and going over them with lawyers until she understood all their subtle differences and shades of meaning. She even wrote an article about them for an academic journal: "Academics were fascinated, because so few of them had agents." Barber is also active in the agent community, and served until recently as president of the Association of Authors' Representatives, its trade group.

After an unfortunate slip in which she failed to notice an obscure foreign rights clause that, she feels, probably cost one of her authors thousands of dollars in lower royalties, she made herself an expert on those too, and now hangs onto foreign rights whenever she can in order to resell them through a network of associated foreign agents. In some cases these have done extremely well for her. Peter Mayle, for instance, who has turned writing about an Englishman's experiences in Provence into a cash machine, came to Barber, through his tax lawyer, many years ago when he was a comparatively obscure author of children's books. Her agency could now prosper on its share of his worldwide royalties alone.

Some clients, like the late MacDonald Harris, do fine work for many years without ever making a big-money career; yet, ironically, in his role as a teacher of creative writing at the University of California at Irvine, Harris was responsible for providing Barber with two of her brightest young stars. One was Michael Chabon, whom Harris sent to her "with a letter full of the most generous praise," and who scored a great success with his first book, *The Mysteries of Pittsburgh*. Another was Marti Leimbach, whose first novel, *Dying Young* was a huge hit (and a not so successful movie, starring Julia Roberts) but who has not been much heard of since.

In her early days Barber tried to find appropriate nonfiction subjects, line her authors up to write them, then doctor their proposals. "The problem with that approach was that you'd get a lot of one-book authors, journalists, people who knew only one subject; and to be a successful agent you need clients who can write many more than just one book."

She is amazed at some of the differences in the publishing scene then and now. "I used to read authors who wrote excellent short stories, and I'd send them away, telling them to come back when they had a body of work. That seems laughable now, when anyone who's ever published one story probably already has an agent." She also finds authors today much more sophisticated in their approaches, less likely than in former times to clutter up the offices with unwieldy manuscripts without querying first. But there's still a lot of mail: "We used to average about ninety submissions a week, and it's probably a bit more than that now." Fiction outnumbers nonfiction proposals by three to one, and most of the successful ones come in by recommendation. They have discovered a few publishable items in the "slush," but it's quite rare. What's usually wrong with the fiction submissions is lack of attention to the need to tell a story, and to dramatize the characters by the action.

The eighty or so authors Barber represents are divided almost equally between fiction and nonfiction, though at one time it was more heavily tilted toward fiction. She still loves finding new talent, "to see where and how far they can go." But she seeks long relationships with authors. "That way you can estimate what someone is capable of, and see how it works out over time." She has some new promising writers she's especially keen about, naming Ixta Maya Murray, David Pilsky, Elizabeth Tippins, and Ann Cummins. Then there are old-timers like Anita Shreve—"She always makes good movie sales, but I expect her to come forward even further as a writer"—and of course Anne Rivers Siddons, who came to her at the suggestion of her Harper editor Larry Ashmead after her longtime agent,

Gloria Safire, died suddenly nine years ago. "You'd better believe I suddenly got a lot more Southern when we talked! Anyway, it worked."

"Editors who are convinced they can make a book work are now routinely shot down by the marketing people."

Although she still bubbles with gusto for the job, Barber has to concede it's more tense and competitive than it used to be. Yes, she's had authors poached away, "but only in a relationship that has really worn out anyway; most of those who have been approached report it to me, and we work it out." But her real problems are with the hustle by the corporate publishing owners for ever higher profits. "They'll pay enormously for big-name writers, okay for brand-new authors they think may go somewhere, but nothing for all those very good writers in the middle. I'm always grateful that Mac Harris died before I had to tell him I just couldn't find a publisher for his new novel—a writer like that!" Too much attention is paid to an author's track record, she feels, and not enough to the manuscript in question. "And even a perfectly decent record won't necessarily help, whereas a patchy one will kill them. I think a publisher should be prepared to stay with an author." And she cites Carol Shields, whom she used to represent, and who was faithfully published by Viking for many years before her career was turned around in 1996 with a simultaneous Pulitzer and NBCC award for *The Stone Diaries.*

"Editors who used to be able to parlay their enthusiasms into an offer, and who are convinced they can make a book work, are now routinely shot down by the marketing people. These people fear there may not be a market, so they're letting their experienced editors' opinions be subsumed by what they *think* the public wants. That's the Hollywood approach, and we've all seen what it's done to the movies."

Other things, too, seem out of proportion to her. "The publishers are cooperating with the chains, who seem to need those enormous stacks of books to pile up. They're terrifying to me, but some authors seem to want it, and even if they don't really have the mass market touch it takes to sell those huge stacks, they'll leave their agents and publishers in search of bigger money, bigger printings."

Barber does see some hope, however, in the burgeoning small press movement and its improved distribution. "We need more small houses like Soho, Graywolf, Jack Shoemaker's new Counterpoint, to publish the kind of work the big houses won't." And she has begun to send books to some of them. "I realize there's not much money up-front, for the author or the agent, but you just can't not have some of these authors published at all!"

WHO: Virginia Barber Literary Agency, Inc.
Virginia Barber; Associates: Claire Tisne, Cornleius Howland, Jay Mandel, Jennifer Rudolph Walsh

WHERE: 101 Fifth Ave.
New York, NY 10003
212-255-6515; fax: 212-691-9418
email: vba@spacelab.net

WHAT: General fiction and nonfiction.

LIST: About eighty clients, split approximately 50-50 between fiction and nonfiction. Does not accept new clients except by referral. Clients include: Rosellen Brown, Alice Munro, Anne Rivers Siddons, Anita Shreve, Peter Mayle, Michael Chabon.

Member of AAR

Loretta Barrett

Loretta Barrett Books, Inc.

In the course of an interview with Loretta
Barrett, she takes only two phone calls: one is from
Faye Dunaway, the other from Janet Leigh, both of
them clients currently working on books. But if the
movie queens of a former era still exert a fascination
for the dark, energetic, fast-talking Barrett, she
doesn't show it. She deals with them crisply, confi-
dently, and reassuringly, much as if she were discussing
with them the possibilities of a new screen role. No,
she hastens to point out, they are not typical of her
client list, which is by no means celebrity driven, and
contains commercial fiction authors as well as a number of serious writers on spiritual themes.

Barrett came out of editorial, and from a much
more prominent position than most agents who
ultimately leave publishing to hang out a shingle.
She went to Doubleday as a young editor, and by the
age of thirty was running its trailblazing Anchor
Books imprint in the early 1970s. "I knew I was in
the right place at the right time." She reels off a roster of legendary names: editor-in-chief Ken
McCormick, publisher Pike Johnson, "and Ann
Freedgood (now retired), Maureen Egen (now publisher at Warner Books), and I ran Anchor together."
Her staff of twenty-two, which included seven or

eight editors, was equally illustrious, and included, at one time
or another, Bill Strachan, now director at Columbia University
Press, the late very talented editor Bill Whitehead, agent Marie
Brown, and editor and author Harriet Rubin. Liv Blumer, now
at the Karpfinger agency, was an assistant, as was star agent Molly
Friedman, now at Aaron Priest, Marilyn Ducksworth, now a
senior vice president at Penguin Putnam, and John Grisham's
editor-agent David Gernert. "We were really troublemakers
for Doubleday," she says with a laugh. "We got into areas they
didn't really want to get into, like the women's movement, the
Vietnam War, but the books sold, so they couldn't complain."

   In the end, however, she found she wanted to be involved in
fiction (Anchor was strictly a nonfiction line), so she moved over
to the trade division as executive editor and senior vice president. Fiction didn't work out at first, and she found herself going
after "high-profile people who were interested in the same issues
I was." These included First Lady Betty Ford, for her alcoholism
recovery book, and television comedienne Betty White for a
book on aging. Her first big fiction success came from an
unlikely source: Barrett's former editorial assistant, Laura Van
Wormer. She had done freelance writing on the *Dallas* and
Dynasty television shows, and wanted to do a novel. "She spent
eighteen months writing away at it in her tiny room, at nights
and on weekends, and when she finished both Betty Prashker (a
fellow senior editor) and I read it, and felt the same: the first fifty
pages were great, then it was awful. And we both urged her to
give up the idea of fiction, since she obviously couldn't do it."

   But Van Wormer ignored them, kept working on her novel,
which turned out to be *Riverside Drive,* the first of a series of
successful novels about life in New York. "We paid her $50,000
for it, it made a big paperback sale and went on to be a big hit.
She's still a client, and I've just sold two new books of hers for
six figures each." There is a moral here that Barrett is keen to
stress, for both authors and agents. "Writers *have* to write.
Although we both told her to drop fiction, she didn't listen to

us and kept at it. And that's one of the mottoes I live by in this business. 'You can tell me no, but you can't tell me I'm wrong.' If you know you're right, you can handle rejection."

In 1987 the giant Bertelsmann group of Germany bought Doubleday, and for Barrett the atmosphere changed. She stayed on for three more years, but "I'd often thought about being an agent. I'd always loved selling as well as buying; after all, I had to sell Doubleday on many of the authors I acquired. And I loved working with authors. I asked friends and colleagues, and they all said it was time." So she set up on her own in the spring of 1990, with just two clients, Laura Van Wormer and Betty White. At first she rented space from Barbara Lowenstein, so she could have access to an agency with foreign connections. Two years later she and agent Ginger Barber found space together, and have shared it ever since.

Barrett got clients mostly through word of mouth: people she had published at Doubleday came along, editors recommended her. "I'd no idea there would be that many referrals. At a big corporation you tend not to think of yourself as a person, but I suddenly realized how many people I'd met and knew." Many of the referrals needed work, and it was the kind of work she was accustomed to doing. "As an editor I'd seen lots of books that were 80 percent there, but needed that extra 20 percent to make them work. I did a lot of that." She also went out to writers' conferences. "I always liked to travel, especially to California, so I'd go out and talk to people and nearly always come back with some project." She had also learned to be patient: "I got used to projects developing slowly over time, and to hanging in there." Ann Douglas's brilliantly reviewed *A Terrible Honesty,* for instance, was a book she had originally signed up at Anchor that took years to finish, and that Doubleday publisher Steve Rubin allowed her to take with her when she left, to sell to another house she thought better suited to it. She also knows, from experience, how much marketing help publishers need, so she never sends a proposal out without a strong marketing sheet. "Authors always know more about the market for a book than anyone else, so they give me the information I can work up into a marketing plan. It's a collaborative effort, but very important."

Barrett's list is comparatively small—about fifty strong—and tilted heavily toward nonfiction, with particular interest in psychology, spirituality (including Zen Buddhism), and conservative ("*not* right-wing!") thought. She had, she feels, a "profile" at Anchor, and sometimes finds, many years later, that authors come to her with a book because of it. Ray Kurzweil, one of the fathers of artificial intelligence, had done a male diet book, but told her he wanted to do something more ambitious: *Age of the Spiritual Machine*, sold recently to Viking for a big sum, was the result. She'd like to do more fiction, but finds it hard to find enough she likes, and doesn't really have time to look because of the amount of work she spends on her nonfiction authors; she's thinking of hiring an agent especially to do it. Apart from Van Wormer, Mariah Stewart, who does commercial women's novels for Pocket Books, is her most prominent fiction client.

"There should always be a natural conflict between editorial and sales. Sales is for today, but an editor should always be looking to tomorrow."

As someone from the heart of publishing, Barrett is extremely concerned about many of the trends she observes now. "The lack of respect and authority given to senior editors is what bothers me most." And she tells the story of an auction where she thought she had complete approval of everyone in the publishing house. At the end she was asked to postpone the final decision, only to be told that, after all, the publisher had found fault with the project. "It was only for $50,000; meanwhile the other bidders were upset, and everyone's time and energy had been wasted." Editors with years of experience, as she sees it, nowadays have very little control over their lists. "They have to get the approval of five or six people to buy anything, and then the decision is often no when they want to say yes. There should always be a natural conflict between editorial and sales. Sales is for today, but an editor should always be looking to tomorrow, thinking of an author's future capabilities. They're simply not being given credence."

But if senior editors are not being sufficiently heeded, Barrett feels that younger ones are out of the loop altogether. "They're not being exposed to the proper experiences, their knowledge of the business just isn't there." Many of them, she asserts, no longer go to sales conferences to present books (which is often done now on videotape, or by the editorial director), therefore they do not have the input, which she and her Anchor colleagues once found so valuable, from the salespeople. "They'd tell us what was selling in the campus bookstores, and we got important authors that way. They told me, for instance, about the success out there of Judy Chicago" and she now represents the artist. She has to wait far too long for editors, especially younger ones, to call back, but doesn't blame them. "They can't get any answers, so they wait until they *can* call with something to tell you."

Yes, she agrees that the delay on getting contracts and payments is "awful—they've cut way back on the number of people in the necessary departments, and the red tape drives me crazy." In so many ways, she sees publishing as going the way of corporate America. "There's this obsession with the bottom line, with ever higher profit margins, and it's so unrealistic. It's never going to be more than 10 percent in trade publishing, and they can do perfectly well with that."

Above all, she is pleased to be out of publishing and into agenting because of her authors. "I don't want to be one of those people who can't do anything for their authors—and editors these days are often powerless on their behalf."

WHO: Loretta Barrett Books, Inc.

WHERE: 101 Fifth Ave.
New York, NY 10003
212-242-3420; fax: 212-691-9418

WHAT: Some celebrity books, mostly psychology, spirituality, political thought, Eastern religion.

LIST: About fifty clients, largely nonfiction. Clients include Betty White, Janet Leigh, Faye Dunaway, Laura Van Wormer, Ann Douglas, Mariah Stewart, Judy Chicago, Ray Kurzweil.

Member of AAR

Vicky Bijur

Vicky Bijur Literary Agency, Inc.

Bijur began in agenting mostly because she was looking for a new challenge in publishing. A slim, dark woman with the compact body and fluid movements of the dancer she originally came to New York to be, she works out of a spacious apartment on West End Avenue in New York from which her husband, a food consultant (and one of her clients as an author) also works.

The move came shortly after she had left Oxford University Press, where she worked for nine years, five of them at a job called preparatory editing—"It was mostly copyediting and getting a manuscript ready for the printer, that sort of thing, looking after everything"—and where she eventually rose to managing editor. But university press publishing felt to her like a dead end, especially after an earlier time in which she had worked on books by the likes of James MacGregor Burns (his book on Edward Kennedy), Edwin Newman, and Kenneth Clark, with a roving freelance editor named Jeanette Hopkins.

So when she met agent Charlotte Sheedy at a party and heard she could use someone in her office, she went to work for her—"and I thought I'd died and gone to heaven." Sheedy, she said, treated her like a full-fledged agent from the first day, even while she was learning the ropes. "She gave me a manuscript and told me that if I liked it I could take the author on. I read it and I did like it." It was by mystery writer Margaret Maron, who went on to become an Edgar winner. "This was in 1986, and mysteries by women were very hot at the time. It was an easy and encouraging time to be starting out."

Then Bijur had a son, and because she needed to work at home, became an outpost of the Sheedy agency in her dining room. With Sheedy's encouragement, she took over more and more of the clients she'd worked with at the agency, and eventually, when she wanted to start on her own, Sheedy called all of them, told them they would be working in future with Bijur, and had Bijur's agency clause sent to them in place of her own. "It gave me an incredible start. I was very lucky."

She has between forty and forty-five active clients, divided roughly fifty-fifty between fiction and nonfiction, including health titles and "serious narrative nonfiction." Science writer and biographer Robert Kanigel is a fine example of the latter, with award-winning and well-reviewed books on the American efficiency expert Frederick Winslow Taylor and Indian mathematical genius Ramanujan; likewise Alice Outwater, with *Water: A Natural History.* An unusual client is Larry Gonick, whose *A Cartoon History of the Universe* was acquired by Jacqueline Kennedy Onassis as an editor at Doubleday, and went through two volumes before her death and then moved to Norton (also becoming a prizewinning CD-ROM along the way). Gonick has become a vastly productive artist, with more in a series of Cartoon Guides (to the environment, statistics, sex) signed through 1999. Bijur also has some writers on health subjects, but has found that publishers now have stopped buying health books by people who do not have medical degrees; in one case, a writer previously published without difficulty could only get a new book accepted after a deal had been worked out whereby the book appeared under the auspices of the New York University Medical Center. A book on breast cancer she could have "easily" sold a few years back no longer finds a buyer. "About seven years ago I began to see things that I could have sold earlier but no longer can." With mysteries, which form a significant part of her list and her income, the story is much the same. "The mystery field has shrunk since I started in 1986," she says. "It's harder to sell now, so I'm very careful about whom I take on." Like most agents, she finds it easier to sell a new writer than an experienced one whose sales have not been at an acceptable level. "A publisher used to support someone for eight or nine books, now they get impatient after four or five"—and since series characters are all-important in such tales, that means authors have to come up with new ones more frequently. Her mystery authors include such stalwarts as Margaret Maron, P.M. Carlson, Susan Rogers Cooper, Susan Holtzer, James Sallis, Laura Lippman, Julie Smith, and Gloria White.

> *"Your focus is on your authors and their careers, not on office politics. You can do everything the way you want it."*

Bijur, as an agent working with only part-time help, finds the flood of new submissions intimidating, and confesses she had herself removed from several agent listings (remaining only in the key *Literary Marketplace* one) to help reduce the flow. "I get most of my new authors through referrals, and I didn't find I was getting any worthwhile submissions through all the listings."

But Bijur still feels lucky to be an agent, despite the often-recited difficulties of slow contracts and slow payments (which are getting slower). "It's something you can do very well on your own. You have to worry only about the books on your desk, not your title, or who has the corner office, or waiting for other people's signatures. Your focus is on your authors and their careers, not on office politics. You can do everything the way you want it."

WHO: Vicky Bijur Literary Agency, Inc.

WHERE: 333 West End Ave. (Ste. 5-B)
New York, NY 10023
212-580-4108; fax: 212-496-1572

WHAT: A strong list of mystery writers, some health, "serious narrative nonfiction."

LIST: Forty to forty-five active clients, about 50-50 fiction and nonfiction. Clients include Margaret Maron, Robert Ranigel, Alice Outwater, Larry Gonick, P.M. Carlson, James Sallis, Laura Lippman, Julie Smith.

Member of AAR

Georges Borchardt

Georges Borchardt Inc.

He is the very model of the dapper Frenchman: slight, always elegantly turned out, witty and world-ly, with a delightful mixture of cynicism about much of publishing today, and boyish enthusiasm about his extraordinary list of authors. He and his wife Anne, who have run the agency together for thirty-eight years ("we're a sort of mom-and-pop store") have a list of more than 250 writers, at least half of whom are familiar names to anyone who reads. It is one that has been built slowly and patiently, with infinite care, from the time Borchardt first arrived on American shores, just after World War II, planning to stay a year to learn the language and then go back to Paris.

This most literary of agents, as he admits, was originally a person least likely to have gone into such a career, since at first, though he had six years of English at school in France, "I could translate Shakespeare but I certainly couldn't conduct a con-versation." He came as a refugee from law school, which he'd found, after a year, that he hated, and "coming here to learn the language was an honor-able way to get out of it." He wasn't particularly interested in publishing, but being virtually alone in the world (most of his family had died in concen-tration camps) he had to support himself, so, "full of optimism," as he wryly notes, he put two differently worded ads in the *New York Times* offering his services as a translator from the French. He got two replies, both from the same person: an author's representative ("I didn't even know what that was") called Marion Saunders. She was the daughter of a British foreign service officer, who knew a number of languages, but loved speaking French, and wanted someone to read some of the new French authors in the original, and tell her if they were worth translating and publishing in the United States. They hit it off at once, but before she agreed to take him on, Saunders said there was someone else she had agreed to see. "That was me, too," he told her, still relishing the joke after more than fifty years.

It was an exciting time in French literature; young authors like Camus and Sartre were coming to the fore, and Borchardt was in on the beginnings of their American careers. He worked with Saunders for four years, then, before even becoming a United States citizen, served a mandatory two years in the Army; in his case it was the Tennessee National Guard, enabling him to wear to his delight, buttons that say "Fustest with the Mostest." Next he was asked by a French publisher, Editions de Seuil, to be their United States representative and he did so, at the same time teaching French at New York University. This lasted another six years, by which time it was 1959; he married Anne and they set up together as agents full-time. He wanted to start taking on English-language writers too, but since he had been known only for his French related activities, that was slow at first. Still, there were notable writers to represent. One was Charles De Gaulle ("pretty heady for one still in his twenties"); there was Samuel Beckett, who wrote in French (and whose estate Borchardt still manages), Eugene Ionesco, Franz Fanon. They were published by houses like Grove and George Braziller, "looked down on by the big publishers, but they did a lot of valuable work at that time."

The Borchardts hired an assistant, Rosemary Macomber, who took on representation in the United States for some

British publishers ("We thought it would give us more credibility in the English-language field") and that brought in writers then just making their names, like Frederick Forsyth and Ruth Rendell. They began to take on writers of their own, looking for high quality: there was Robert Coover, Stanley Elkin, Sol Yurick, George Steiner (whom Borchardt had known as a child growing up in Paris). Elie Wiesel came in through his French publisher; "He was very hard to sell at first, but now he's worth a great deal." And he talks with glee of the reselling of the expired paperback license of Wiesel's classic *Night,* turned down by many publishers at first, with hefty bids coming from some of those same publishers. The same thing still constantly happens, as in 1997 with Andre Makine's prizewinning French novel *Dreams of My Russian Summers,* which was turned down by many big houses before being published by little Arcade; paperback rights recently went to Pocket Books for six figures.

Borchardt represents David Guterson, whose *Snow Falling on Cedars* turned out to be a phenomenal success in 1996 and 1997. "Everyone is looking for the new Guterson, but anyone could find him. You have to be persistent. It's often hard, slow work." He recalls how Guterson was brought in by Anne Borchardt; she liked his short stories, which sold about two thousand copies. Then he did a nonfiction book on home schooling, "which did okay." *Cedars* received "a very timid offer" from Harcourt, which had an option, and Anne took the book to two other publishers, who turned it down, before letting Harcourt have it, with results now known around the world; the book is in twenty-two languages and a movie is on the way. "The public is often more astute than the publishers these days," Borchardt comments. He adds that he can hardly ever predict a bestseller among the books he represents, "except perhaps once, with Jane Fonda's workout book."

He and Anne go often to writers' gatherings, more because they enjoy the company of writers than in search of new talent, though they do actively seek it out. "If we didn't the agency would be less vibrant, life would be duller; it would be just a matter of negotiating contracts for writers we already have." And he notes waspishly that "some agents just specialize in authors who are already famous; those deals are easy to make. The hard thing is to develop your own tastes and instincts." A number of their current clients have sought them out because of the quality of their list, much as many writers yearn to be published by Knopf: some examples are younger writers like T.C. Boyle, William Boyd, and Susan Minot.

"I don't take on an author just to bring in money, or drop him if he doesn't. There are many books and authors that don't bring in much, but I don't see it as wasteful."

They or their assistants—there are now six of them, with varying responsibilities—do not read unsolicited submissions. "I suppose there are six a day, and we take on perhaps six a year." Most of their new clients are recommended by other writers, though "some have better taste than others, and some are just getting rid of pestering students." Sometimes editors suggest they take on someone who has approached them, though "that doesn't necessarily mean we'll sell the book to that editor."

Though Borchardt's is thought of as an essentially literary list, it is surprising to discover that he estimates that two-thirds of his authors are nonfiction writers, including one or two decidedly nonliterary ones like C. David Heymann (*A Woman Named Jackie* and other scandal-laden celebrity biographies). Although many of his clients are well-known, and many of them bring in high commissions to the agency, Borchardt seems to think about the financial aspects less than most agents do. "I don't take on an author just to bring in money, or drop him if he doesn't. There are many books and authors that don't really bring in much, but I don't see it as wasteful." And he tells a story about Robert Coover and how he had written an Op-Ed piece for the *New York Times* (for the usual fee of about $200), which the paper decided, at the last moment, not to run as it was written. Coover was deeply disappointed, and Borchardt spent the entire weekend making calls and sending faxes until he got the piece accepted instead by the *Los Angeles Times*. Someone asked what he had received for all that work and time, and when Borchardt told him it was about $20, "he couldn't understand it." He explains: "A good agent will do things for his authors because they need to be done, not just for the money."

Not that the agency isn't highly profitable. It occupies a large suite of bright, book-lined offices on an upper floor on one of the most expensive blocks of Manhattan's East 57th Street. "I pay a lot to be here because I figure we spend most of our time here," he says with a smile. Their apartment is much smaller, and with many agents he thinks the priorities are probably the other way around.

No take on Borchardt would be complete without a hint of the riches of his client list: In alphabetical order, it includes not only the names already cited but John Ashbery, Louis Begley, Robert Bly, Andre Brink, Jerome Charyn, Stanley Crouch, Arthur Danto, Joseph Epstein, Mavis Gallant, Gary Giddins, Francine du Plessix Gray, Barbara Grizzuti Harrison, Molly Haskell, Charles Johnson, Donald Keene, Tracy Kidder, Richard Kluger, John Lahr, Alan Lelchuk, Ian McEwan, W.S. Merwin, Jack Miles, Kate Millett, Edmund Morris, Francine Prose, John Rechy, Ned Rorem, Richard Selzer, Ted Solotaroff, Daniel Stern, and dozens of others equally distinguished.

To handle them all, Georges and Anne work closely together, though at opposite ends of the office, consulting from time to time. "We don't see each other much during the day. But we enjoy sharing an exciting social life—our relationships with our authors are very close."

WHO: Georges Borchardt Inc.
Georges Borchardt, Anne Borchardt, Rosemary Macomber

WHERE: 136 East 57th St.
New York, NY 10022
212-753-5785; fax: 212-838-6518

WHAT: General fiction, mostly literary, and a wide range of nonfiction, including biography, history, belles-lettres, poetry, contemporary affairs.

LIST: About 250 clients, including many literary celebrities, two-thirds nonfiction. Clients include John Ashbery, T.C. Boyle, William Boyd, Louis Begley, Robert Bly, Andre Brink, Robert Coover, Mavis Gallant, David Guterson, C. David Heymann, Donald Keene, Tracy Kidder, Ian McEwan, W.S. Merwin, Kate Millett, Edmund Morris, Andre Makine, George Steiner, Elie Weisel.

Carl D. Brandt

Brandt & Brandt Literary Agents Inc.

This is one of the oldest agencies in New York and Carl D. Brandt, who has been here for forty years—much of that time in an office perched on a high floor of the Times Square building that used to be the Paramount Building and the Astor Hotel—is an old-fashioned man in the warmest meaning of the word. Big, burly, shirt-sleeved, and humorously taciturn, rather like a captain of industry who has read a book or two, he starts off with the kind of line that makes an interviewer's heart sink: "An agency is a silent service. I don't believe in being a public figure." As it turns out, however, he is perfectly willing to talk as long as he is not expected to be loquacious or waste any words.

The firm is one of the two or three oldest (probably predated only by Paul Reynolds) and was launched shortly before the First World War by a woman named Mary Kirkpatrick, "who actually hired my father to sweep the floors. She disappeared after the war, and he took over, and brought in my uncle. The uncle was a very straight arrow, and my father was not, so it was obvious my uncle wouldn't quite do as an agent, and he went off, quite rightly, to be an editor at the *Saturday Evening Post*." For the next thirty years the agency, like most at the time, was concerned largely with sales to magazines; the notion of agents for book authors grew much more slowly, though the firm did acquire some very notable clients in the 1940s and 1950s, including Mignon Eberhart, James Gould Cozzens, J.P. Marquand, and *Freddie the Pig* author Walter Brooks (whose work, Brandt is delighted to note, is about to be brought back by Peter Mayer at Overlook Press).

Then in the 1950s the magazine market began to vanish under the onslaught of television. "There were probably thirty or forty writers making $50,000 a year out of magazine work, which was serious money then. They were losing their livings; it was very sad." And this was just about the time Brandt himself was joining the agency, as a matter of family urgency. He had been a newspaperman, then worked for *Look* magazine. "I was a boy reporter at the 1954 Geneva Conference, loved the idea of minding other people's business. I could have been a decent reporter, but I'm afraid I was a pedestrian writer." But his father was dying, his younger sister needed to go to college, "so I did what I felt I had to do and went into the family business." He at once brought in some fellow journalists, "trying to fill the hole, and the hole was pretty damn big." Another source of new writers was a series of Latin American conferences he attended in the early 1960s which, long before the Gabriel Garcia Marquez phenomenon, brought in writers like Carlos Fuentes (still with him), Jose Donoso, and Cabrera Infante.

He picked up other clients on recommendations from authors or from editors, whom he describes as "schizophrenic people—they're paid by their bosses, but their essential sympathy is with the writers. They'll sometimes send writers to you so they can blame the agent when they face unpleasantness against the author." A link with British agency A.M. Heath brought in British writers like Sarah Gainham, Winston Graham, and Anita Brookner. Brandt's own interests are largely in nonfiction, especially journalism and history (his clients include Stephen Birmingham, Joseph Lelyveld, Stanley Kauffmann, John Toland,

Robert Kaplan, Terry Tempest Williams, and Geoffrey Ward). He
is one of those proactive agents who has ideas for books which
he then pitches to an appropriate author, then, of course, to a
publisher: "That's what those lunches are all about!"

He credits much of the agency's current very strong fiction
list to Gail Hochman, now a full partner, who joined about thirteen years ago after working at Putnam and then the John
Hawkins agency. "She is just terrific at fiction," and numbers
among her many illustrious clients Scott Turow, Michael
Cunningham, Ursula Hegi (given a huge lift by an Oprah book
club choice), Scott Smith (*A Simple Plan*), and National Book
Award–winner Bob Shacochis. Hochman does go to writers'
conventions, and is ever on the lookout for fresh talent. And
Brandt approves: "We get set in our ways, it's useful to go out
and listen to other ways of doing things—maybe even listen to
ourselves talking."

> *"Publishing is the only industry left where
> delayed gratification is a necessity, an essential
> part of the business, and the new financial guys
> don't seem to understand that."*

Brandt says they will always read a letter outlining a submission and reply ("if it has stamps for return") but will under
no circumstances accept manuscripts; "we just refuse them."
There are probably 100–150 submissions a week, more than ever
these days, "now the computer makes everything look so neat
and well-presented, I think it doesn't do the authors any favors,
because they confuse an elegant-looking first draft with finished
work." And despite all the electronics, he finds all the publishing
processes slower than they used to be.

Unlike many agencies, Brandt's has a drama side, the Robert
A. Fredman Dramatic Agency, with which it shares overhead; but
on the literary side, apart from Hochman, there are two agents,

Marianne Merola, who is "coming along brilliantly," and beginning to work with clients, though not yet to bring them in, and Charles Schlessiger, who began many years ago as a secretary to the legendary Bernice Baumgarten.

Brandt's thoughts on the state of publishing are succinct. "It's the only business left where delayed gratification is a necessity, an essential part of the process, and the new financial guys don't understand that." His pet peeve? "Grandiosity is the worst thing about publishing now. I always had the feeling that publishing is at heart a true cottage industry. Important and useful things got done at a sales level of ten thousand to fifteen thousand copies. It even used to be possible to make a little money at that level, and still is, with smaller publishers. But now there's so much money going into the overheads, into the desperate search for that big book, that they've lost a sense of what they're supposed to be doing."

WHO: Brandt & Brandt Literary Agents Inc.
Carl D. Brandt; Associate: Gail Hochman; Agents: Marianne Merola, Charles Schlessiger

WHERE: 1501 Broadway
New York, NY 10036
212-840-5760; fax: 212-840-5776

WHAT: General fiction and nonfiction, about 60 percent in favor of nonfiction.

LIST: About 230 clients, who include Stephen Birmingham, Anita Brookner, Michael Cunningham, Nicholas Delbanco, Carlos Fuentes, Winston Graham, Ursula Hegi, Stanley Kauffman, James Alan Macpherson, Joyce Maynard, Bob Shacochis, Scott Smith, Richard Martin Stern, John Toland, Scott Turow, Jerome Weidman.

Marie Brown

Marie Brown Associates

Marie Brown is a disarmingly gentle, soft-spoken agent who occupies a pair of small, cluttered offices on lower Broadway; she is also one of only two significant African-American agents in New York (there are a handful elsewhere in the country). As she says, she "sort of backed into it" after various stints, as a teacher, an inter-group education coordinator, a book editor, a magazine editor, and a bookseller. "I never thought I wanted to be an agent, but writers convinced me I was needed," she says.

As a teacher in Philadelphia after college, later as a coordinator in the Philadelphia school system, she was asked, in the late 1960s, to come to New York and talk about her work to then-editor Loretta Barrett and others at Doubleday. "Loretta took me to *lunch*," Brown says, savoring the country-innocent angle, yet making it clear that it had indeed seemed like a big deal at the time. But it turned into more than a book discussion meeting. "That was sixties affirmative action time, and Doubleday offered me a position as publishing trainee." That lasted nearly a year, then she spent two years as Loretta's assistant. She moved to Los Angeles for two years, then returned to Doubleday as an associate editor. This time the job lasted nine years, until 1981, and when she left it was to work on a magazine start-up. From there, "I resumed my affair with the book world," and took what she thought would be a temporary Christmas job at the Upper West Side's classy Endicott Booksellers, now no longer extant. "In the end I stayed two years, and became Susan Bergholz's assistant manager and assistant buyer."

Meanwhile, writers and editors she knew, particularly African Americans, were urging her to take the plunge into agenting. This was at the time, she says, when it was becoming far more necessary to have an agent to get taken seriously by publishers; "In the old days we'd take far more over the transom. Some people told me: 'You're not mean enough,' and maybe they were right, but I thought I could do it in my own style; and I thought of all the contacts I had with the people still at Doubleday, or who had passed through there and gone on to other houses—there would always be someone I could call, so there was some comfort level there." Her old colleagues at Anchor, including Barrett herself and Gerald Gladney, all turned out to be early customers. Even Jacqueline Onassis expressed interest in one or two projects, "though I never actually sold her anything." She started working out of her home, while still keeping her job at Endicott on a part-time basis to pay the bills. "But then I found I was getting too many calls at work, driving Susan crazy," so in 1984 she quit as a bookseller and became a full-time agent.

"As an editor I was used to doing the rejecting, and I found I hated to be rejected. I used to dread seeing those jiffy bags come back and open them and find the rejection letters."

She had to do everything at first, spending too much money on stamps, jiffy bags, and copying, and found it extremely hard going. "I would meet my clients in coffee shops so I didn't have to take them home." She also found it psychologically tough. "As an editor I was used to doing the rejecting, and I found I hated to be rejected. I used to dread seeing those jiffy bags come back, and I hated to open them and find the rejection letters." For eight years she struggled on in this way, accumulating new clients—"not only black authors, though there were a lot at first"— and their manuscripts. Meanwhile, Brown was supporting the agency with various consulting stints. "Back in the eighties a lot of publishers began doing African-American books, but they didn't know how to market them, so they'd call me in." She worked at one time or another in this fashion for Workman; Stewart, Tabori & Chang; Algonquin; Ballantine's One World Press; and Doubleday.

Finally, in 1992, Glenn Thomson, publisher of Writers & Readers, Inc., told her about office space downtown, and she moved in. She now has one full-time and one part-time assistant, and, acknowledging that she probably took on too many people while she was building the agency, is trying to "downsize a bit, to the point where I can handle the right number to bring in the level of income I need." She has about fifty active clients, with a preponderance of nonfiction, and about 25 percent in children's books. She does a few writers' conferences and panels, mostly on the East Coast, where as a minority agent she is something of a novelty. She tries not to accept too many new people, but does take a look at all the unsolicited material she gets. For the proposals that work for her, "there's a lot of time that has to be spent getting it to the point where I can send it out." Authors can be frustratingly naive about this. "One told me recently that an editor won't care about the details of the proposal because he's a great promoter, but they *will* care. We have to convince authors that, especially these days, they have to revise until it's the best it can be, and not leave it to the editor."

Authors she is particularly proud of include Susan Taylor, a Doubleday author; Gwendolyn Parker, author of *These Same Long Bones,* and *Trespassing,* a memoir, both published by

Houghton Mifflin; Randall Robinson, whose memoir *Defending the Spirit,* is doing very well for Dutton; Sharon Robinson, Jackie's daughter; Faith Ringold, an exceptional children's author and illustrator, whose *Tar Beach* won a Caldecott award; another children's author, Tom Feelings; Donald Bogle, author of a recent biography of Dorothy Dandridge; Tonya Bolden, a prolific children's writer; and Helena Maria Viramontes, an award-winning novelist.

Brown sometimes feels that she isn't really cut out for the business in some ways: "You have to be adventurous, and go out and meet people; it's a very social business. And since I know I can't compete with the really pushy people, I have to learn to sell my way. But if you establish your own style and method of working with editors, and I have now, it can work out for you. I find I now get good responses from many editors, though there'll always be a few who never call back, and with fiction I find you have to really nag people."

She has an unusual problem in that African-American writers, especially women fiction writers, have been so fashionable lately. "At one time any promising new black writers seemed to expect to get a quarter of a million automatically, and I don't get those sort of advances for literary fiction. I lost clients. But often they didn't work out, and some come back to me, but what can I do for them then? It's too late." She says she doesn't like to oversell a client, no matter what the temptation. "If they get a big advance that doesn't work out, the word gets out that you oversell, and next time the editors will resent you. For many writers one big advance is it, then there's no more. But the ones who learn to wait longer, if they earn out their first advance, they'll have a better chance of making a bigger deal next time, and maybe begin to build a career."

She tries always to identify editors very carefully by what she knows interests them. "When you get one of those impersonal rejections like 'It is the feeling here that...' chances are it means their colleagues don't trust their judgment; and I find books often work best when they're an editor's book, something they feel strongly about." Yes, she gets some authors poached away, particularly in the competitive field for African-American titles these days. "But it's a problem to hang on when someone with more clout, or seemingly more persuasive powers, comes along. I've had people I've launched who became disenchanted because they felt I didn't get enough for them this time out, or their friends tell them about how other agents do things. One author left because I didn't FedEx everything, like she'd heard someone else did." She laughs bitterly. "She couldn't find anyone else."

But Brown really cares, despite her rather self-effacing gentleness, and she says, without a trace of the hype with which some people in publishing say similar things: "I can survive, and even be optimistic, because I love the industry, I love what we do, the relationship with books and authors. If I didn't feel that, I couldn't be in it, although it's sometimes so disheartening."

WHO: Marie Brown Associates

WHERE: 625 Broadway
New York, NY 10012
212-533-5534; fax: 212-533-0849
email: mbrownlit@aol.com

WHAT: General fiction and nonfiction, strong on African-American interest, some children's books.

LIST: About fifty clients, mostly nonfiction or children's. Clients include Susan Taylor, Gwendolyn Parker, Randall Robinson, Sharon Robinson, Faith Ringold, Tom Feelings, Donald Bogle.

Knox Burger

Knox Burger Associates Ltd.

Burger is a lean, bald, craggy-faced man with a game leg which he assists with a cane, an expression usually either amused or sardonic, a gruff manner that can sometimes seem downright brusque, and a reputation as one of the truly upright men in the business. Almost alone among agents, he does not believe in signing contracts with his clients: "I don't want to represent someone who doesn't want to be represented by me, and if either party really wants to split, a contract doesn't mean much."

He began, after service in World War II, in the magazine business, as an editor at *Collier's*. There he came to appreciate good short fiction, and still recalls those buccaneering times with some fondness. Then he was in on the early days of mass market paperbacks, working with such pioneers in the field as the late Donald Fine and Ralph Daigh. The reason he got into the agenting business, he says, was that he couldn't make enough money as a paperback editor, didn't have hardcover book experience and therefore could see no prospect of improving his salary, and so decided the best thing was to work for himself.

He started out in the basement of a small apartment building just off New York's Washington Square, where he lives on the fourth floor. He took

over what had been the super's apartment as an office; eventually, as the agency prospered, he expanded, though his offices,
where he works closely with his wife, Kitty Sprague, and an
assistant, are still only a few steps down the street.

---

*"Agents took more and more power through the
seventies and eighties because they cared more
about their clients and the actual writing than
the editors did."*

Early clients were people he had known from his magazine
and paperback days. He'd hoped that Kurt Vonnegut and John D.
MacDonald, both of whose early fiction he had purchased
before, would be among them, and they had indicated they
planned to join him; but in the end circumstances dictated otherwise (the wife of their agent at the time died, and they decided that was no time to leave him), and "Boy, did my heart sink!
I started out well behind the eight-ball." Burger says he "had the
notion that the only way to make money on my authors was to
help shape their careers, and have a say in the way they were
sold." It didn't work out quite that way, though he feels that
"agents took more and more power through the seventies and
eighties, because they simply cared more about their clients and
the actual writing than their editors did." And many editors did
not have Burger's keen sense of what worked and what didn't,
particularly in crime fiction, which has always been his strong
suit (a friend describes many of his clients as "thick ear" writers,
an English phrase that delights him).

His first real success was with an old friend, Mort
Freedgood, writing as John Godey, whose regular publisher was
Random House, and who wrote hard-boiled thrillers with a
dash of comedy (a favorite genre of Burger's). After a succession
of expert but rather slight stories, Godey had written a more
ambitious and obviously very commercial thriller about the

heist of a New York subway train, called *The Taking of Pelham One Two Three*. He had been offered his usual advance, $3,500, by his Random editor, but Burger was deeply convinced the book was worth much more. He showed it to an editor at Putnam and got a high five figure advance (this was back in the early seventies), and the book went on to become a big bestseller and a successful movie. But only after Burger had applied some of his editorial know-how: "I talked Mort into reducing the scale, from a whole crowded train taken over by an army of brigands, to four men taking over the lead car carrying only a handful of people."

Another of his major successes is Martin Cruz Smith, who was publishing, not very successfully, with a low-end mass market house before he came to Burger. "I give varying amounts of editorial advice, according to the author. Smith showed extraordinary potential, but he was writing very fast for very low advances, which resulted in frequent chaotic passages. It took years before we got to *Gorky Park*." The rest, as they say, is history.

A couple of Burger's other most successful authors, the classic crime writers Lawrence Block and Donald E. Westlake, came over in part because their former agent raised his commission to 15 percent from 10 percent. (Burger varies his commission according to how much work he has to put into a project; in the case of Block and Westlake it's at the lower end because he sends their beautifully crafted books out "as is.") These two are both vastly productive, each with several series heroes to their credit, each producing at least one new book a year, and each with a string of movie sales.

In addition to his "thick ear" authors, Burger also has a handful of literary authors, critics, and essayists for whom he works just as diligently, finding them sometimes small and scholarly publishers for not much money, and for whom he works hard at getting critical attention. "I call that my pro bono stuff," he jokes gruffly. "Would you believe I represent the world's leading authority on John Milton?" He also represents the estate of a man who showed him how to apply lubricating oil to the mechanism of a swivel chair when Burger was an office boy at *Time* magazine, and who later became better known as James Agee.

Burger has almost no female clients. "I don't know why," he says, with what seems genuine bewilderment, but which is probably a sly joke. "I don't seem to have much feel for women's fiction. Or fantasy, come to think of it." He represented Nancy Friday's first book—the idea of she and Burger strikes one as a mind-boggling combination—"but she sent in outlines I just didn't believe in, and we parted company."

For anyone who has been around as long as Burger, it's almost inevitable that many aspects of publishing will seem to have declined in quality from the old days. "There are far too many editors around who simply don't know enough about what they're supposed to be doing, and it's hard to respect them," he says. "Also, as an old pro, I bitch a lot to publishers about their ads, their promotional materials. There are a lot of authors around now seeking representation who've been previously published but simply don't feel they were being well represented or published. And sometimes they're right."

Due to his great seniority, he says, he is taking on almost no new clients.

WHO: Knox Burger Associates Ltd.

WHERE: 39 1/2 Washington Square South
New York, NY 10012
212-533-2360; fax: 212-677-3170

WHAT: General fiction and nonfiction, 60 percent fiction, mostly thrillers.

LIST: About thirty active clients, including Lawrence Block, Donald E. Westlake, Martin Cruz Smith.

Member of AAR

Linda Chester

The Linda Chester Literary Agency

Having scored a spectacular success with Wally Lamb, whose career was made when Oprah Winfrey chose his novel *She's Come Undone* for her book club (the first male author she had chosen), and then went on to anoint him a second time for *I Know This Much Is True*, Chester is understandably feeling expansive. She is in fact remodeling and expanding her midtown offices, and therefore meets her interviewer in a swanky Upper East Side hotel for afternoon tea, no less.

She is an attractive blonde woman, carefully made up and dressed, who treats each initial encounter with caution. As the talk proceeds she seems to unwind and relax, so that some of the rather pompous statements she made at the start of the interview ("What distinguishes us is our personal involvement in every aspect of publication" and "We're noted for our gentleness and kindness") seem in retrospect to have been the product of nervousness.

Chester began, like so many others, in the Doubleday training program, with an initial leaning toward publicity, a function she clearly still understands thoroughly. Then she moved to California, but found "not much doing" (these were early days on the California book scene). She called Nelson Doubleday to seek his advice, and he asked her whether she had ever considered being an agent. She hadn't, but when she met agent Julian Bach, and he expressed interest in an affiliation, she went to work there. She could bring in her own clients, but only got a third of the commissions they produced, so after a few years with Bach she went off on her own. That was about eleven years ago, beginning with an office in La Jolla, California. That office has now moved to Berkeley, and her main office has shifted to New York.

From the start, Chester says, she has been extremely proactive (the "personal involvement in every aspect"), specializing in bringing subjects and authors together. "We get lots of submissions from friends, lots of cold calls, but in the end I think the best projects are the ones we created ourselves." This would involve the conception of the idea for the book; the finding of an appropriate writer; the editing, often with outside freelance editors involved; the designing; and the use of an outside publicist when the book comes out—in many ways it sounds more like packaging than agenting. The "gentleness and kindness," Chester says, even goes as far as taking female clients who are visiting the city out shopping.

Chester figures she has sold about two hundred books in the time she's been agenting solo, at a rate of fifteen to twenty a year, these break down to about 35 percent fiction to 65 percent nonfiction, with half of the latter "things we've arranged." The "we" includes Laurie Fox, who runs the West Coast office, Joanna Pulcini, and Judith Ehrlich (the latter an author as well). Other authors they represent include Jonathan Kirsch, Mark Sullivan, and Janet Wallach.

She found Wally Lamb after reading a short story he published in a literary magazine. "I wrote him a fan letter and asked him if he was working on a novel. He said he'd be glad to talk if I was willing to critique it. It turned out several agents had approached him, and he'd told them all the same, but he liked our critique the best." Chester says she worked with him for a while on *She's Come Undone* before it was submitted. It's not uncommon to spend a lot of time shaping a submission, but more common with nonfiction than with fiction. Nonfiction proposals, she says, often go through five or six rewrites before being submitted. "Proposals have to be really outstanding, but then the publisher today still needs a pre-sold personality, with a built-in readership. I don't know of any other industry where people expect to have everything handed to them on a silver platter. Most editors aren't actually editing any more, and we'll often agree to get an author his or her own editor, after acceptance, to polish them up."

Even in her comparatively brief time agenting, Chester has noticed striking changes. "Some of my early books seem kind of embarrassing; I'd never have sold them now." She still has some offbeat authors and titles, like one called *Book of Shadows* by Phyllis Curot, whom she calls "a wicca witch," which she defines as "a spiritual witch" (sold to Broadway as a lead title, and with $250,000 in foreign rights already sold) and a book by a man with multiple personalities, *First Person Plural,* who actually treats other people similarly afflicted. Published by Hyperion, this has been sold to Robin Williams for a movie in which he will be both director and star. She hastens to add, however, that these are not typical, and "I don't want to do a lot of such books." The main thing, she feels, is that "you have to believe in the author."

"With the right author, it's a reasonable idea to have them share more in the profits, since they do the work."

As to publishers, she has the common impression that they "care more about the bottom line than the quality of the book or the author," but would like to see some new approaches to advances and royalties, perhaps along the lines of those recently worked out with Stephen King and Clive Cussler. "With the right author, it's a reasonable idea to have them share more in the profits, since they do the work." She also feels publishers should not accept returns of unsold books: "That way the authors would get their royalties quicker." (As it is, the publishers normally hold back payment of a portion of the royalties against the possibility of returned books.)

Chester is pleased with the way her agency has grown, but would like to see even more expansion. "You can't stand still in this business, you have to keep planning for what's next, and, yes, worrying a bit about it too."

WHO: The Linda Chester Literary Agency
Linda Chester; Agent: Joanna Pulcini; Associate: Judith Ehrlich; West Coast Associate: Laurie Fox

WHERE: 630 Fifth Ave.
New York, NY 10111
212-439-0881; fax: 212-439-9859
email: lcagency@aol.com

West Coast Office:
1678 Shattuck Ave. (Ste. 331)
Berkeley, CA 94709
510-704-0971; fax: 510-704-0792

WHAT: Books often packaged as subjects with particular authors in mind; strong emphasis on nonfiction (65 percent). Unsolicited material not accepted except by reference.

LIST: About forty to forty-five active clients, producing twenty to twenty-five books a year. Clients include Wally Lamb, Jonathan Kirsch, Mark Sullivan, Janet Wallach, Phyllis Curot.

Faith Childs

Faith Childs Literary Agency Inc.

Growing up in an upper-class, well-educated, landowning black family with a lifelong sense of entitlement, having a household always full of books, and attending a prestigious law school—all this was part of the background of Faith Childs, who has emerged as one of the key African-American agents in the country, at a time when there has been increasing interest in the sort of books she represents.

Beautifully spoken, with a strong intelligence that comes through with charismatic intensity, Childs seems much younger than her fifty-some years. She is slight, with a shaven head and fashionable glasses—of which, she says, she has two pairs, one for looking at the computer, the other "for common discourse." Her speech is full of little literary turns of phrase which might seem pretentious were they not utterly unconscious, and her favorite word seems to be "precisely"—uttered whenever her interviewer seems to have caught her shade of meaning just as she intended.

She was raised in Washington, D.C., with, she says, "no notion of what I wanted to be when I grew up." Her parents were English teachers, her father a keen book collector, and she had always read deeply and widely, "the thread in my life." She went to law

school, at American University, "for the wrong reasons"—largely, she thinks, because her mother had wanted to be a lawyer but
law schools then didn't take women. She actually practiced, in
three different cities, for ten years, "but I was never interested in
it and it didn't work"—though it did give her a solid knowledge
of contracts. Her introduction to the notion of agenting came
through a friend in a book group who knew agent Jed Mattes.
"I knew lots of writers, and this seemed like something I could
do." So Mattes sent her to Charlotte Sheedy, and she apprenticed
herself to Charlotte for four years. "I was thirty-five and I wanted change; it was one of those 'Belle of Amherst' moments. I
wanted to enter a life of the mind."

She felt that it also meant a change of personality. "I would
have to give up my normal nature, which is terribly shy; I needed to be the opposite, to go to parties, confront people, sharpen
all the pencils!" Although Sheedy was having a hard time
making a go of it at first, this didn't faze Childs, who felt "it
couldn't apply to me; meanwhile I had to learn how business was
done." Her first nine months there she didn't sell a single book.
Eventually she felt she couldn't continue to function with a mentor ("It was a 'slay your father' kind of thing") and went off on her
own, working at first out of a spare bedroom in her apartment.

Her first years were "lean," but "I had savings, I was not without resources, and I put everything I made back into the business.
If you take a salary you only get taxed on it anyway." Her first
break came when a highly regarded black author, Paule Marshall,
was leaving her agent, and asked to meet with her. She sold the
book, *Daughters,* to Atheneum, and this made a difference, she
says, in terms of her visibility. She had about twenty-five clients
then, and "worked very long days." But with the flowering about
ten years ago of African-American literature, things began to
shape up, though there were still problems of perception in the
white readership. When she tried to sell a memoir by a young
black man who went to Boston Latin and Harvard, she ran into
a wall. "I couldn't sell the experiences of people like myself.

Emblematic of the black experience was poor, ignorant, and dangerous, violent, naked, complaining. It's easy to sell a book like *Up from Slavery*, because people are comfortable with that. But sophisticated, well-to-do black people in the middle or upper class are very difficult for people to relate to."

In the end she created what she calls a "highly integrated" list, though "people I've never met would call me up and send me black, just because I'm black. That's somewhat frustrating, but," she grins, "not overwhelming." She adds: "I don't want to be Balkanized. The trigger is, will I be interested? Not the color of the writer."

"We now buy BSOs—book-shaped objects—the same way we buy bedsheets or ice cream, at these huge stores. A publisher takes someone who's not a writer and tries to sell a book by that person because they're a successful actor or hairdresser, or whatever."

Her integrated list now consists of about seventy-five clients, balanced about 60-40 in favor of fiction, and includes James Ridgeway and Sylvia Plachy of the *Village Voice*, Thulani Davis, Suketi Mehta (a "wonderful book on Bombay" sold to his namesake at Knopf), Derrick Bell, James Alan Macpherson, and two prolific mystery authors, Jill Churchill and Valerie Wilson Wesley. "There's a quality slant to the list," she comments. "If it looks like a mystery, there's some social history in there too." She is particularly keen on biography, and has recently sold ones on Alice Walker and Richard Wright, and her author David Leeming is doing an unauthorized study of Stephen Spender.

She works with university presses (a social history of single-mother families), as well as with some small presses, both here and in the United Kingdom. Sometimes she suggests books to her authors ("I have lots of ideas"), and sells a good number of movie and television options—"You can option almost anything." She feels the book business has changed most in the "kind of mercantilization that has crept in; we now buy BSOs—book-shaped objects—in the same way we buy bedsheets or ice cream at these huge stores. A publisher takes someone who's not a writer and tries to sell a book by that person because they're a successful actor or hairdresser or whatever. I suspect there's that infection everywhere: it's easier to take on what looks like a success than groom a writer, and build on a ten thousand- or fifteen thousand-copy sale." As she notes, there's no market research in publishing, "but it's full of shibboleths as to what will or won't work."

She wants to nurture her writers, but finds to her sadness that whatever she can do doesn't always work: "Sometimes the book comes through beautifully, sometimes it takes what seems like too long, and people remain underappreciated. A true writer, as opposed to someone writing just for money, never gives up, however; they care about their craft." She tells her writers they have three lives to live: "A life to write, a life to promote what you've written, and a life where you do what you have to do to sustain the others."

She feels the change in editors in recent years can be seen in comparing the rejection letters on file now and ten years ago: "The recent ones are very short." And she finds she often misses the continuity of having the same editor who bought the book also work on it; "trying to get a second editor up to speed is just too difficult." There is "rather a monocular quality to editorial decision-making now, a rather limited range of interests. Is it them or their corporate surroundings? We need to expand the breadth of what we buy, especially in foreign literature."

Still, notwithstanding that the industry is "going through a sort of duck press," she still maintains her enthusiasm for taking an author "through the first baby steps, getting him to an enthusiastic publisher. It still happens often enough—there's at least one book like that every season—to make me hopeful."

WHO: Faith Childs Literary Agency Inc.

WHERE: 915 Broadway
New York, NY 10001
212-645-4600; fax: 212-645-4644
email: faithchil@aol.com

WHAT: General list with emphasis on quality; concentrating on fiction (60 percent), biography, Third World subjects of special interest.

LIST: About seventy-five clients including Thulani Davis, James Ridgway, Derrick Bell, Suketi Mehta, James Alan Macpherson, Sylvia Plachy, David Leeming, Jill Churchill, Valerie Wilson Wesley.

Member of AAR

Don Congdon

Don Congdon Associates, Inc.

Don Congdon is a remarkably tenacious survivor from a storied generation of agents, with an astounding array of big names in his past. Some of them are still active, and for others he handles their estates, but their names include William Styron, Thomas Berger, William L. Shirer, Ray Bradbury, William Manchester, Lillian Hellman, Russell Baker, Jack Finney (*Time and Again*); more recent clients include Ellen Gilchrist and David Sedaris (*Naked*).

Congdon is an elderly man, now in his late seventies, with white hair, a bushy mustache and the genial charm of an old actor. He greets his interviewer at the end of the day with a fine Scotch malt whisky, and sits sipping a large tumbler of Johnnie Walker scotch, well watered, throughout the interview. He loves to talk about his celebrated clients, gets embroiled in stories about them which sometimes makes it difficult to bring him back to the present and keep on the point. But a conversation with him is always full of fascinating glimpses of a legendary past.

He began work in 1936 as a teenage messenger at the long-gone Lurton Blassingame agency at $12 a week. Jobs were hard to find then, and "I guess I got it because I typed less badly than some earlier candidates." He would take manuscripts around by hand to the various publishing houses. He stayed with Blassingame for eight years, during which he started working with a few writer clients. Having learned a fair amount about how the business worked, he was lured to *Collier's* magazine, then in its heyday, to help edit fiction. After a couple of years it was on to Simon & Schuster as an editor, where he was particularly interested in the early post–World War II novels. His boss, Dick Simon, was never very interested in fiction, so Congdon had a hard time getting novelists to come to the house. However, he had read early stories about a family called Caulfield, which a young writer called J.D. Salinger was contributing to the *Saturday Evening Post*. He got in touch with Salinger via his agent, Harold Ober (he recalls them going together to hear Billie Holliday) and tried to sign his first book of fiction, which turned out to be *Catcher in the Rye,* for Simon & Schuster. He actually got as far as having Salinger's contract on his desk, but Salinger wasn't willing finally to sign the deal, calling S & S "a smart-ass publisher." Eventually he took the book to Harcourt Brace, but because they wanted changes he wasn't prepared to make, it went in the end to Little, Brown.

Later Congdon quit Simon & Schuster to work for agent Harold Matson. "I didn't have any clients to bring him, and I wondered if he'd have enough for me to handle. He really didn't, and for the first five years it was tough, partly because Matson prevented me from soliciting writers." It was the early 1950s and "the movies weren't buying much, and book publishers were pulling in their horns." It took seventeen years of steady list-building before Congdon recorded his first big success, but it was very big indeed: William Manchester's 1965 *The Death of a President,* about the Kennedy assassination, for which he got a modest advance but a colossal first serial sale to *Look* magazine. "It was $665,000, and I believe it is still a record for serial rights."

That was the same year Matson's nephew Peter joined the agency; another major development was Matson's acquisition of the McIntosh McKee and Dodds agency, which had the makings of a good list that included William Styron. "Matson had a rule about not going after clients, but I admired Styron's work, and I persuaded him to come with us." Other big successes during the Matson years included David Reuben's *Everything You Wanted to Know About Sex But Were Afraid to Ask,* a huge bestseller in the seventies that is now largely forgotten; it was, says Congdon, "one of the first books that was made by television. Carson had Reuben on, and the night of his interview sales jumped tenfold; it sold a million hardcover copies over the next twelve months." Davis Grubb's *Night of the Hunter,* which made a brilliant movie, was another favorite of his. Shirer's *The Nightmare Years* made big money for a television miniseries, and another of his authors, Charles Williams, was always a big seller overseas. Ray Bradbury was, and remains, a perennial favorite science fiction writer, though his work seems to Congdon more fantasy than science fiction.

Though Congdon worked with Matson for thirty-five years before leaving to set up his own agency in 1983, it was never a partnership—Congdon worked on a sliding-scale commission basis—and he is still distressed at the fact that "we couldn't put it together." In the end (like Peter Matson, who went to Sterling Lord), he had to go his own way. Meanwhile, he had been joined by his son Michael, who still works with him and has his own list of clients.

These days Congdon makes a lot of his revenues on movie sales, he made three big movie deals last year, including one with Mel Gibson for a remake of Ray Bradbury's *Fahrenheit 451.* But, he says, "you can waste a lot of time at it. They'll walk you to the altar but never say the vows." He's still talking to Miramax about a possible movie of Russell Baker's *Growing Up* after more than fifteen years. Unusually among agents today, he also likes magazine sales: "With a magazine assignment, if a writer is reasonably important, you can insist the price be guaranteed if the manuscript is delivered, whether they use it or not."

Congdon has actually written a book, which he finished last year, about some of his celebrated clients, telling stories about them and his dealings on their behalf. Agent Richard Curtis, he says, offered to send it around. "Some of the top editors said kind things about it, but that doesn't mean they were willing to publish it. I guess they thought it was too specialized for readers outside the business." At present he is offering it to university presses. Though Congdon is obviously disappointed at the general lack of interest in his tales, he notes, apropos his own book as well as many others, "You can send a manuscript out to fifteen places, and get fifteen different responses."

"What's really hurt mid-list fiction, decent fiction as opposed to the genre stuff, is the absence of mass market paperbacks. Those sales used to make all the difference in a publisher being able to spend for a book."

Despite his long career, Congdon likes to be in touch with younger writers, and seems to have a good eye for them (David Sedaris was sent to him by old friend Roger Donald at Little, Brown), and he eagerly peruses the submissions. "If someone writes a letter I like, I'll call right away." Two new writers he has just taken on include the author of a novel about a young woman's experiences in the New Guinea jungle, and another who did "a fascinating rewrite of *Tale of Two Cities.*" He loves, he says, to give advice on a writer's first or second book. "That way I can help a writer get more respect from editors, because new writers can't go directly to publishers anymore, they have to depend on agents to get their work considered."

He agrees it's a hard time for first novelists, though he notes that more subsidiary rights are possible in fiction than in most nonfiction, including foreign and movie rights. "What's really hurt mid-list fiction, decent fiction as opposed to the genre stuff, is the absence of mass market paperbacks. Those sales used to make all the difference in a publisher being able to spend for a book."

Congdon still likes the business, but complains that "old properties take so much time—and there's so much crap being published these days."

WHO: Don Congdon Associates, Inc.
Don Congdon, Michael Congdon, Susan Ramer

WHERE: 156 Fifth Ave. (Ste. 625)
New York, NY 10010
212-645-1229; fax: 212-727-2688
email: doncongdon@aol.com

WHAT: General fiction and nonfiction.

LIST: About sixty active clients, emphasis on fiction.
Clients include William Styron, Thomas Berger, Ray Bradbury, Russell Baker, Jack Finney, Ellen Gilchrist, David Sedaris, and the estates of William Manchester, William L. Shirer, Lillian Hellman.

Member of AAR

Richard Curtis
Richard Curtis Associates, Inc.

Curtis's very name strikes terror and resentment into many publishers, who see in him the embodiment of the agent as "knife at a publisher's throat," in the old adage. A bearded man with a darkly saturnine expression, a sinister chuckle, and a strong New York accent that is oddly endearing when used to express, as it often is, complex and eloquently formulated thoughts, Curtis delights in a description once given of him as "the velvet shark." He keeps on his desk, in fact, a Beanie Baby representing just such a creature.

Almost uniquely among agents, Curtis seems to have a solidly constructed philosophy of the publishing business and where it is headed, a sometimes cynical, sometimes crusading vision he feels himself impelled to help fulfill. This elaborate construct contrasts oddly with the nature of his list, which until recently was strongest in genre fiction: romance, science fiction, horror, even Westerns, but has now, in response to what he sees as the currents of the marketplace, done a U-turn in the direction of nonfiction.

Curtis has a very strong sense of the current power and significance of agents, and has been in a position to see it grow, even helped it to do so.

"Since World War II the publishing market has been more and more agent-driven, to the point where it's quite beyond belief the extent to which authors and publishers are *less* significant than the agent." When he speaks at writers' conferences and gatherings, which he often does, it is to declare ringingly that "the most important person in the publishing process is the agent. No decision is made without consulting the agent, or trying to figure what the agent is thinking. That's the way the business is being run. It's just a fact of life."

Unlike many in the book world, interest in things literary came late to Curtis. It was not until he had graduated from high school and was about to go to Syracuse University that he had what he calls his "awakening," when several schoolmates asked him a series of "probing philosophical questions" he was embarrassed to be unable to answer. "I suddenly became a bookworm, went from zero to the classics in months, fell in love with Henry James, edited the school magazine, where I published Joyce Carol Oates's first story. I didn't understand her then, and I don't understand her now." Wanting to be connected somehow to the literary life, he answered an ad that took him to an interview at the Scott Meredith Literary Agency. Meredith was a remarkable figure, an agent driven obsessively by greed, who made his fee-reading services a cash cow that quite overshadowed the rest of his work, but who was also a considerable innovator; at the time of Curtis's arrival, in the late 1950s, he was at the height of his powers. Curtis got the job by successfully editing a deliberately and horribly inept story written especially by the late Lester Del Rey to test the editing abilities of applicants. Curtis was hired, he says, to handle foreign rights, "though I didn't even know what a right was," and in his seven years at Meredith built it into a multimillion-dollar department. When he left in 1966 to become a full-time writer, building on the experience of writing overnight magazine assignments and potboilers to supplement his meager Meredith salary, he wrote a huge instruction manual for his successors, who turned out to be Ralph Vicinanza (now Stephen King's agent for foreign rights) and Russ Galen, now a partner in an agency that took over most of Meredith's clients after his death.

"Those were great, palmy days, fun days," Curtis says. "A lot of things now taken for granted in agenting started back then: scouting for foreign publishers, foreign auctions. Everything he developed, including multiple submissions, was trailblazing at the time." But despite his swashbuckling impact on the genteel publishing mores of his day, Meredith, Curtis remembers, had a bitterly dark vision: "Authors were babies who just wanted to be fed, publishers were exploitative sons of bitches who had to be kicked or they would kick you." Curtis pauses, with a sardonic grin. "I vowed when I started my own agency that I would work on the opposite principles: that authors were responsible adults who should be treated as such, that the more you gave publishers the better they would treat you. Now I wonder whether on the whole Scott was more right than not, but it's still not in my nature to follow his principles and act on those beliefs."

"I enjoy resolving opposing forces, creating some Hegelian kind of synthesis. At one time I actually thought of going into professional diplomacy, believe it or not."

For a time after he had formally quit, Curtis maintained his association with his old boss, offering to help him keep up with his correspondence by writing letters at a dollar each, even going to England to open up a Meredith outpost there. Then, in the late sixties, he began to make a living as a writer. "I did sex novels, quite innocuous ones, some thrillers, some kids' books, a lot of collaborations." Altogether, he figures he wrote forty or fifty books in five or six years. "At Meredith you could do a book a month; I trained myself to write at that speed, and I could still do it if I wanted to." But although it was a living, the freelance life took its toll, and when an old Scott Meredith client asked Curtis to represent him he did so, and others followed. At first it was a farcical situation. "I literally had two desks, an author desk and an agent desk, and a swivel chair between them. For years I tried to do both, but when the phone would ring I would always answer. I guess in my soul I was cut out to be an agent, and eventually the cheap currency drove out the dear one." But it wasn't only a question of money. "I enjoy resolving opposing forces, creating some Hegelian kind of synthesis. At one time I actually thought of going into professional diplomacy, believe it or not."

When he turned to agenting full-time, Curtis, ever the joker, printed up letterhead saying "The One Horse Literary Agency"—the one horse at the time being historian T.R. Fehrenbach, author of *Lone Star,* which Curtis considers the best one-volume history of Texas ever published. He incorporated in 1979, and soon other authors began to arrive, "some disaffected ones from other agencies, then referrals." John Jakes, later to make a huge success with his North & South trilogy, was an early client (at that time a fantasy and science fiction writer). For a time Curtis shared office space with another agent, Susan Ann Protter, and in 1982 he bought out a leading science fiction agent, Robert Mills, whose business was slipping. After the takeover, Curtis says, he realized that the acquisition of another company in the book business means "basically the taking over of a set of filing cabinets containing contracts and copyrights." Overnight he became a major player in the science fiction field, with stars like Greg Bear, Harlan Ellison, Dan Simmons, and R.A. MacAvoy. The Mills agency acquisition also yielded the estate of the late Jim Thompson, which became a rich lode of lucrative book and movie deals. As romance became more mainstream, the ever market-savvy Curtis added that to his list of specialties too, consolidating by landing Janet Dailey, for whom he signed a number of multimillion dollar contracts (long before she became embroiled in a long-running plagiarism case).

He also became, increasingly, a public spokesman for authors' rights. For twelve years, from 1980–92, he contributed a regular column to *Locus,* the newsletter of the Science Fiction Writers of America. Out of these, Curtis ultimately compiled two published books designed to help authors through the publishing maze, *How To Be Your Own Literary Agent* and *Beyond the Bestseller.* He also became active on behalf of the science fiction writers, helping them organize audits of publishers whose royalty reports they believed, often with good reason, to be less than just. In fact, he says with mock solemnity: "If anyone wants to chisel something on my tombstone, I'd like them to say that 'Here lies a person who raised consciousness about royalties.' I think I succeeded, to the extent that royalties are now better reported than they were."

Just in case he seemed to be acquiring too bright a halo, however, Curtis acknowledged that for a time he, like Meredith, had run a fee-reading service for would-be clients. Honestly done, he avers, it can unearth good clients. Still, he gave it up after a time. "Meredith had it down to a smoothly running machine, but I found it simply too cumbersome to make it profitable," he said. "The last reason I gave it up was because it was immoral," adding impishly: "It's simply too hard to be moral all the time." Another odd tactic he engaged in was to advertise for new writers in the *New Yorker* magazine, on the theory that *New Yorker* readers were unlikely to be hopelessly inept. He actually got one or two clients that way, but gave up, he said, because it cost too much.

When electronic publishing began to raise new possibilities in the early 1990s, Curtis became an active proselytizer on behalf of authors to "ensure they didn't get screwed in this new world." He takes credit for introducing a concept now widely adopted by agents, that whereas publishers could retain certain print extensions of the written word for electronic use, multimedia use of the material is essentially an extension of movie rights and therefore rights should be reserved to the author.

On the agency side, he had seen the writing on the wall for some time about the collapse of genre mass market publishing, in which most of his clients were heavily involved, and, deciding "I had to reinvent the agency," he turned in the past few years from 80 percent fiction and 20 percent nonfiction to the reverse proportion. Fiction now, he says, has a solid core of his star authors, whereas the much larger list used to have more range. Fiction still brings in more money, because of the size of the names, but most of his attention is now focused on market-driven nonfiction.

Ever one to change with the times, Curtis says he has long envisaged a time when people would read from hand-held electronic devices rather than books. He tried to invent one himself, but now that he has been beaten to the punch by well-financed technology firms, he's working on strategies to help authors develop their potential in the new electronic media. "The collapse of the publishing structure and the rise of on-line means it's only a matter of time." (He claims he was, incidentally, the first agent to create a Web site.) The industry's continuing pursuit of a paper-based medium is, he declares, a waste of time and resources when a reader can download and read anything written, cheaply and easily, "and the day has to come when that technology will rescue the publishing business, the writing business, and literacy."

WHO: Richard Curtis Associates, Inc.

WHERE: 171 East 74th St. (Ste. 2)
New York, NY 10021
212-772-7363; fax: 212-772-7393
email: 75152.3677@compuserve.com

WHAT: General fiction and nonfiction, with emphasis on genre fiction.

LIST: About one hundred active clients, current emphasis on nonfiction. Clients include John Jakes, Janet Dailey, Greg Bear, Harlan Ellison, John Bellairs, Poppy Z. Brite, William C. Dietz, estate of Jim Thompson.

Member of AAR

Liz Darhansoff

Darhansoff & Verrill Literary Agency

Alone among agents, Liz Darhansoff is way out of Manhattan's normal commercial zones, with offices on a side street near the Hudson River way downtown in TriBeCa. And her clients are inclined to be out of the usual easy commercial run too, though with the recent flare of interest in strong literary fiction she has enjoyed some startling successes. Annie Proulx won both the National Book Award and the Pulitzer Prize for *The Shipping News,* Charles Frazier's *Cold Mountain,* represented by Darhansoff's colleague Leigh Feldman, was the first-novel sensation of 1997 and 1998, and Kaye Gibbons received the inestimable benefit of an embrace from Oprah's television book club. So it seemed as though the Darhansoff & Verrill agency's boast, printed on its client list, "Peddling Quality Literature since 1975," did not have as hollow a ring as it once might have had.

Darhansoff, a friendly, relaxed woman whose offices, as might be expected in her neighborhood, run to brick walls, heavy beams, and dark corners, came from a part of the publishing business not often heard from in agenting: publicity. An art history major at Hofstra, she answered an ad and, as she puts it, "fell instantly in love with the business." Her first job was as a publicity assistant at Atheneum, only five years after the launch of that once distinguished, now defunct house. She was there for two years, learned to care for authors and traveled for a while, then went to Random House in a similar capacity. "I found I liked literary books, and doing publicity for people like Stanley Elkin and John Barth. It was a great time." She has a thought. "In those days I was in on the end of the book publishing process. Now I'm in at the beginning, and this is really more exciting."

After seven or eight years of her publicity work, Lynn Nesbit at ICM called and asked whether she'd be interested in joining the agency, and she did so in 1973. She was working alongside a lot of celebrated agents, and quickly learned the ropes. She still recalls her first sale. "Monica McCall dropped a manuscript on my desk, a big Scottish-Irish family saga, a first novel. I sold it for $5,000, then it went for $100,000 to paperback. It seemed easy! But I realized I really didn't want to be part of a big agency. I wanted to make my own choices, which were always going to be, first and foremost, literary fiction." So she left in 1975 and started her own agency, working at first out of her home, with a nucleus of about twenty writers she had taken with her from ICM.

Very early on she built a list of talented Southern writers, partly through her friendship with Louis Rubin, pipe-smoking founder of North Carolina's Algonquin Books of Chapel Hill. They included Lee Smith, very early on, later Kaye Gibbons, Jill McCorkle, Clyde Edgerton, Larry Brown. Charles Frazier eventually joined (in 1993, four years before the book he had been working on for so long was published to such national acclaim) as part of that connection, too. Other noted clients included William Kennedy, who had been a book reviewer and who had often sent her potential clients. "One day he said 'How about me?' so I took him on." Everything eventually turned around for Kennedy with the success of *Ironweed* and the decision to bring his earlier, less successful fiction back into print. Peter Kramer joined later, represented by partner Chuck Verrill, and ultimately had a tremendous hit with *Listening to Prozac.*

Her new clients come in mostly through referrals, often from editors, sometimes from other authors, though Darhansoff does read submission letters from unknowns. Her interest in illustration accounts for the presence on her list of people like Nick Bantock (whose *Griffin and Sabine* was a huge success for Chronicle Books in San Francisco and has had several successors), Lynda Barry, and Bruce McCall. Serious nonfiction is represented by, among many others, Taylor Branch, author of the monumental biography of Martin Luther King, striking regional fiction from the West by Harriet Doerr and Ivan Doig.

"It's a great time for literary fiction, for those for whom it's all working, but unfortunately there are plenty of writers once done by publishers like Knopf and Farrar, Straus, but who now have to be published, if at all, by little houses, and I worry about that because small houses can't afford to give them what they need."

How long did it take for the agency to actually start making money, to take in more than it was paying out in rent, phone, copying and mailing costs, part-time help, and so on? "They said it would take three to five years, and it did."

Naturally, given her list, Darhansoff finds it "a great time for literary fiction," though she quickly qualifies that. "It's a great time for those for whom it's all working, but there are unfortunately plenty of writers who were once done by publishers like Knopf and Farrar, Straus, but who now have to be published, if at all, by little houses like Milkweed. I worry about that because small houses can't afford to give them what they need." (She knows authors who have changed their names so they can start again as if they are first-timers, without any record of failure hanging over their heads.) She also worries because many authors' books are now on bookstore shelves for a much shorter time than they used to be, in the endless hustle to shovel out new "product," and about the number of writers whose books get "orphaned" at their publishing house, as the original editor who signed the book and cared for it moves on, and the book is left without an advocate.

Darhansoff sees the taste of individual independent booksellers as the great hope for good books—"those wonderful people who have such good instincts." One of her recent successes, Jan Karon, author of the popular Midford series, was first spotted by independent booksellers when she was only being published by Lion, a small religious house. When Darhansoff took her on, she moved her to Penguin and bestsellerdom.

What she would really like, she says, is to be able to select the exact right editor, who can see what she sees in a book and author, and who would give her a response in about three weeks—"but I haven't been able to do that in a good while." Yes, every response is slower these days: replies, money, contracts. She has a thought about the current difficulty editors seem to have in making up their minds. "I think some editors, who may not be absolutely confident in their judgment, want to feel they're in a contest with someone for a book; at least that way they know someone else has read it and liked it, and they're not entirely on their own, sticking their necks out."

Darhansoff's fellow agent Charles Verrill (a former Penguin editor who represents, among others, Peter Kramer and Anne Lamott and who edits Stephen King) became a partner in the early nineties. The agency has about one hundred active clients today, with a distinct tilt toward fiction. Apart from Darhansoff and Verrill, there is agent Leigh Feldman, and Kristan Lang, who handles rights along with Catherine Lutting.

Darhansoff is old-fashioned enough, she says, to believe in the agent's conciliatory power between author and publisher. Recalling the old joke that "the agent is to the publisher as the knife is to the throat," she laughs and exclaims, "Never!" then adds: "It's our job to make things work out the best they can between the two of them."

WHO: Darhansoff & Verrill Literary Agency
Liz Darhansoff, Charles Verrill; Agent: Leigh Feldman

WHERE: 179 Franklin St. (4th flr.)
New York, NY 10013
212-334-5980; fax: 212-334-5470

WHAT: General fiction and nonfiction, with a tilt toward literary fiction.

LIST: About one hundred active clients, including Annie Proulx, Charles Frazier, Lee Smith, Larry Brown, Jill McCorkle, Kaye Gibbons, Clyde Edgerton, William Kennedy, Peter Kramer, Nick Bantock, Anne Lamott, Taylor Branch, Harriet Doerr, Ivan Doig, Bruce McCall, Lynda Barry, Jan Karon, Arthur Golden.

Member of AAR

Sandra Dijkstra

Sandra Dijkstra Literary Agency

"Sandy," as she is universally known in the book publishing business, may live and work in one of the more laid-back parts of the country—her office is in Del Mar, north of San Diego—but few agents are as strenuously energetic, even ruthless, on behalf of their clients. Dijkstra—she acquired the name from her Dutch husband Bram, who is also a client—is ubiquitous at book events. She will turn up at a book party for a client, three thousand miles away from her office; she is a regular at all the book fairs; and she never loses an opportunity to push a client and, not so incidentally, her agency. She is one of the very few agents who occasionally gets profiled in the consumer press, and soon after her interview for this book (which took place in a chic Italian restaurant in Greenwich Village, where the interviewer, lingering over drinks, was succeeded at the table for dinner by one of the hotter young New York editors) a package was delivered that contained a sampling of her press clippings.

Dijkstra is a lean, fiercely intense woman of around fifty with close-cropped hair, a big smile, a throaty voice, and a strongly persuasive presence. Born in New York, she moved out to California, took an M.A. in Comparative Literature at Berkeley, a Ph.D. in French Literature at University of California San Diego and, fully intending to become an academic, was on a tenure track at the University of Virginia. Then her husband (whom she met and married when they were both students at Berkeley) decided to return to his job at UC San Diego. Dijkstra became what she called a "vagabond academic" for a few years, finished her dissertation (on feminism and George Sand) and sought publication of it in New York. When she said she was going to see New York editors, a friend gave her a proposal for a book on the history of "romantic friendship between women" to shop around. "I left a copy of the proposal with Ann Freedgood at Random House, with whom I had corresponded about my dissertation. Descending in the Random House elevator I met a subsidiary rights person from Morrow, who took me to see editor Maria Guarnaschelli there, who said she was interested." Another visit was to Loretta Barrett at Doubleday. She was away that day but her assistant Elizabeth Knappman was willing to talk.

The year was 1978, and a new career was about to be born. "On hearing about me and my friend's project, Elizabeth told me I should try being an agent. I didn't know what an agent was, but I soon learned that anyone can hang out a shingle. It was when Freedgood asked what I wanted for the proposal that the idea came to me: Lots of friends were writing books—why don't I try agenting? I thought then, and now know better, that the only word an agent needs to know is a four-letter one, 'More.' Before I knew it I was conducting a phone auction in my kitchen. Maria won and I thought: This is easy. I can write my own books and sell books for my friends. I soon learned that agenting was a more complicated business than that."

But before she could settle into a new life, two things happened. She got a big job offer from UCLA, and her mother became ill and died, leaving her some money. For a time she hovered between the two occupations, teaching and doing a little agenting on the side, from an office in her bedroom. She started a radio show called *Books West,* in which she interviewed publishing people and writers who came to California, got to know people like Betty Prashker at Crown and Marty Asher (now Vintage chief, then at Simon & Schuster). That helped her visibility, and on her next trip to New York, "I was surprised that important editors like Alice Mayhew would see an unknown agent like me." Meanwhile, while Dijkstra was still teetering between two careers, her mother's money ran out and "I was attacked for my radical ideas by a right-wing campus newspaper, and the climate of fear was such that no one at the university came to my rescue. By that time I was getting some interesting submissions and I decided to abandon academe and become an agent. It was 1983."

> *"You have got to be passionate about your books and authors. Your job is to identify talent, then package it. You have to be a salesperson of ideas."*

At first it was tough going. She sent out rather academic submissions, and they all came back, but the editors, including the late Erwin Glikes, were so encouraging that she kept going. "However, I did begin to wonder if I could really do this from California." The arrival of Harcourt Brace Jovanovich (as it then was) in San Diego gave her some encouragement, though at first she simply wondered whether, if the agency didn't work out, she could get a job there. "Then I buckled down, got serious, hired an assistant, and began to turn things around. I had heard a new agent can expect a negative cash flow for the first five years. For me it was only two or three."

The essential element in agenting, for Dijkstra, is "to have the courage of your convictions" (the title of a book she later sold by Peter Irons). "You've got to be passionate about your books and authors. Your job is to identify talent, then package it.

You have to be a salesperson of ideas." She feels she is lucky because she has a strong editorial bent—"I have an obsessive blue pencil and a good sense of language." Her academic background helped, she feels. So did the fact that she had no publishing background. "Never having been in the business, I had to imagine it. I always work hard at the publicity side myself, and not knowing the rules I can break them." She took one of her prize clients, Amy Tan, to the American Booksellers Association convention, for instance, before her best-selling *The Joy Luck Club* was published, when the publisher hadn't planned to do so.

The story of how she made Tan into a star twelve years ago gives a good idea of the combination of imagination and chutzpah with which she works. She had read a story by Tan in *Seventeen* magazine, and, as is her wont, called her to see if there were any more like that. Tan told her there weren't, but Dijkstra said she would like to represent her anyway, and the author remembers thinking she must be rather naive. At Dijkstra's regular prodding (weekly calls), she wrote two more stories and sent them in, then went on a trip to China and forgot all about it. When she returned she got a call saying she had three offers—for a book. On the basis of those three stories, Dijkstra had secured her a very considerable advance for what turned out to be one of the big sellers of the decade, *The Joy Luck Club*.

Dijkstra's list carries a number of Asian-American writers, many of them referred by Tan or lured to her by Tan's success; Anchee Min, whose *Red Azalea* was a big hit and made a large movie deal, is a representative one. Lisa See's *Flower Net* was an Edgar nominee. Her list also features Diane Mott Davidson, famous for her culinary mysteries. But alongside the big fictional successes, her clients, roughly one hundred of them, run two-thirds nonfiction. There's a combination of self-help (Debra Waterhouse's *Outsmarting the Female Fat Cell*), inspirational titles (Sue Bender's *Plain and Simple*), and more serious nonfiction. "It's easier than fiction, in the sense that you find a need and fill it," Dijkstra says. She sometimes suggests themes to authors, but "much less than I'd like" because she is so busy with handling their own suggestions—though she did help steer another client, Susan Faludi, to doing what she really wanted to do rather than what she thought she should do: in her case, the bestselling *Backlash: The Undeclared War Against American Women* instead of a guide for single women.

There are a number of history titles by the likes of Eric Foner, David Landes, Mike Davis, and Kevin Starr. On the business side are Max DePree and Harriet Rubin and she is also proud of her growing list of New York–based journalists, including *Newsweek's* Veronica Chambers, *Cosmpolitan's* Kate White, John Richardson from *Esquire* and Chester Higgins of the *New York Times.* She takes on the occasional children's book: the award-winning and best-selling *Stellaluna* by Janell Cannon, came in unsolicited, and Dijkstra recalls that author and publisher disagreed on the text, so she took both versions to several children's bookstores for their verdicts and the author's won.

Dijkstra is indefatigable at selling foreign rights, and estimates that they account for about a third of her multimillion-dollar sales in any given year. She has a wide knowledge of foreign publishers, unusual in an American agent, though she works through other subagents abroad. Dijkstra explains that before or after the Frankfurt book fair each year, she goes to a different foreign country and spends about a week there calling on local publishers; as a result she manages to arrange overseas tours for many of her authors. Despite her proximity to Hollywood, and a number of movie successes for her clients, "we are focused East on the book business; Hollywood chases us."

She has a staff of five, all of whom help read the slush pile "in search of gold." She used to worry about her remoteness from the New York scene but now finds it an advantage. She feels there's a dearth of time-wasting lunches, and though the working day is longer (you have to start on the phone much earlier to catch New Yorkers before they go to lunch), "you in the

East are already asleep while we are still thinking brilliant thoughts." People who once advised her to move to New York are now urging against it, and "contrarian that I am, this advice worries me."

She has some of the same worries as other agents about the publisher delays in signing contracts and paying money—"They do everything in their power to slow the process down." What bothers her even more, however, are the closing windows of opportunity. She mentions an editor at HarperCollins who no longer does biographies, another at Simon & Schuster who now calls fiction "the f-word." And she is concerned that so many seem unwilling to buy "small" books any more. "That's just so shortsighted. They *have* to buy small books. Small books become big books."

WHO: Sandra Dijkstra Literary Agency

WHERE: 1155 Camino del Mar (Ste. 515C)
Del Mar, CA 92014
619-755-3115

WHAT: General fiction and nonfiction, with a strong emphasis (about two-thirds of the list) on nonfiction.

LIST: About one hundred clients, including Amy Tan, Anchee Min, Lisa See, Eric Foner, Susan Faludi, Harriet Rubin, Chester Higgins, Mike Davis, Janell Cannon, Diane Mott Davidson.

Member of AAR

Jane Dystel

Jane Dystel Literary Management

Jane is a thorough book business professional who bears a legendary name: her father, Oscar, led Bantam Books through the years when it redefined mass market paperback publishing and developed one of the strongest teams of editors and marketing people ever seen in American publishing. Jane was part of that team, working for editorial director Marc Jaffe in the program—unique for the time in mass market publishing—devoted to publishing original works.

Dystel is a petite, intense woman, carefully coiffed and made up, whose office, in an airy top floor suite in a building that houses a furniture store on the corner of New York's Union Square, is lined with portraits of her authors. She offers a glossy brochure about "Jane Dystel Literary Management," as she calls her company, which lists about 140 clients, their books and interests, and says of Jane that she has "a reputation for honesty, forthrightness, hard work, and real commitment to her authors and their careers. Her editing skills are exceptional, and she is very savvy about publishing trends. She is also a tough and fair negotiator."

It's a formidable list of qualities, and there seems little doubt that she has had a more varied and com-

prehensive publishing career than most who switch into agenting. She went to Bantam after starting, but not completing, law
school. During her time there she headed the permissions
department in the original publishing program for three years,
learning about rights and contracts. Then in 1973 she went to
Grosset & Dunlap as managing editor. Five years later, after the
birth of a baby girl, she moved on to World Almanac as publisher, and launched its World Almanac Publications. She essentially
ran the company for eight years, "and that's when I got most of
my experience: public relations, distribution, I did author tours,
I planned lists, I learned financial planning." It was a great
grounding for any kind of publishing job, but in 1985 Dystel
tired of it, "and went looking for a job where I could make
money and have fun—and not have any inventory!" she adds
with a shudder.

> *"I guess I'm very aggressive. My father taught
> me you have to pursue things."*

She met the agent Jay Acton (at one time famous as Tip
O'Neill's representative), who taught her, mentored her as an
agent, and brought her into his firm. She worked for the first few
years as an employee, but after 1991 got her name on the door
(as Acton & Dystel) and began to build a list of her own. "Jay
gave me some clients, whom I still have, but, more importantly,
he showed me how to find my own." She went off on her own
in 1994, and is therefore one of the newest agencies in this book.

Her methods include reading widely in newspapers and a
variety of magazines, writing letters, making "cold calls" to people who have appeared in stories or have written them. She calls
it "sowing seeds," and describes how, a few days before her interview, a young novelist had written an Op-Ed piece in the *New
York Times* describing how he had spent his own money going
on tour on behalf of his mid-list novel. "I called him, and of

course he had an agent already, but if ever he should want to change, he'll remember that call." She adds: "I guess I'm very aggressive. My father taught me you have to pursue things."

She got one of her prize clients, young Asian-American novelist Gus Lee, by that kind of pursuit. At a writers' conference in Tulsa (she does go to them), she had met a West Coast writer who, once again, already had an agent; but she kept in touch, and the man, who worked in the District Attorney's office in Sacramento, eventually wrote to say he had a colleague who had written a novel. Would she take a look? The manuscript was *China Boy,* which she quickly sold to Dutton. Another client, Thomas Moran, the former managing editor of *W* magazine, had written a novel that remained unsold after forty tries. She asked if he had anything else, and he came up with a book called *Man in the Box.* She sold it to Riverhead, and in the year before it was published (it eventually won its author a special Book of the Month Club award for best first novel) sold two more by Moran, each for a higher sum than the previous one. "I never give up," Dystel declares. "I believe in my clients, and I want to make sure they get through."

Her client list is strongest in nonfiction, with a particularly powerful list of cookbook authors—"important for my bread and butter." A cookbook was among the first books she sold, among the twenty-odd she marketed in her first year alone: "Then, it was a case of the blind leading the blind," but now she has a number of significant food writers, and links with restaurants and cooking schools that lend their names to new collections. She estimates they may make up as much as a third of her nonfiction list. "There's a very defined group of cookbook editors you sell to."

Other areas of special interest include self-help, where she has a couple of star authors in Elaine St. James (*Simplifying Your Life*) and Stephanie Winston (*Getting Out from Under*). She has an interest in true crime, but finds that currently it's not a strong category. But in all areas, Dystel is actively building the list and refining it as she goes to what she thinks works best.

Fiction is not altogether neglected. It is now about 20 percent of her list, but Dystel would like to get it higher, and has in fact retained her father, chafing in retirement, to go out and scout commercial fiction for her—"He's out there looking all the time." She looks hard too, and says she finds more promising work in the slush pile than most agents will admit to. Every fiction submission has three readers, she says: an outside one, an inside one (usually vice president Miriam Goderich, her in-house editor), and Dystel herself. "I still keep hoping to find that great first novelist." Because she is eager to help young writers develop (and turn into top-selling ones), she has developed a kind of mini–book club within the agency's staff of five, including a new agent plus a bookkeeper. Every month they gather to evaluate each novel currently on the best-seller list, "what we like about it, what we don't like, why and how we think it made the list. We learn a lot that way about what we're looking for, and what we think publishers and readers are looking for."

Another outreach effort is a newsletter sent three times a year to a carefully chosen list of about eight hundred people—editors, television and movie folk, foreign rights agents—describing what's happening at the agency.

Dystel has less complaining to do about the current state of publishing than most agents. "I guess it's because, as an agent, I've never known it any other way." She is very determined and organized, usually sending out multiple submissions, and following up rapidly. "I get fast responses because I insist on them. I say I will call in a week and I do."

The big problems, as she sees them, are the contraction in the number of major publishers, and the instability of many of their staffs. "People move so quickly, and that's very disquieting. And I'm afraid too many young, smart people are getting discouraged and leaving the business."

WHO: Jane Dystel Literary Management

WHERE: One Union Square West
New York, NY 10003
212-627-9100; fax: 212-627-9313

WHAT: General nonfiction (about 80 percent), with a strong emphasis on cookbooks and practical books, some fiction.

LIST: About 140 clients, including Gus Lee, Thomas Moran, Elaine St. James, Stephanie Winston.

Member of AAR

Nicholas Ellison

Nicholas Ellison, Inc.

Nick Ellison offers an unusual persona for an agent: compact, florid, richly bearded, he exudes a kind of swashbuckling confidence and an air of hearty bonhomie, and it is no surprise to learn that quite early in his life he was a professional boxer who won twice as many fights as he lost and was paid he said "in the high three figures" for a fight. He has, however, a far more literary background than that.

He has been a top editor at the old Thomas Crowell company, at Minerva Editions at Funk & Wagnalls, at Harper & Row, where he worked closely with the legendary Cass Canfield, and finally, beginning in 1980 at Delacorte, where he was editor-in-chief under Ross Claiborne. This extensive experience, Ellison thinks, has given him an excellent sense of an author's worth: "I can read both difficult literary fiction and highly commercial fiction, and see where the author is headed, where he'll be ten years from now."

Finding it too hard to work twelve hours a day at his publishing job and still commute to his Connecticut home to spend what time he could with his two children, Ellison quit in 1985 to form his own agency. Right from the start his biggest star,

Nelson DeMille, was with him, having followed him from the publisher. "We've got a lot in common and we're good friends," says Ellison, and indeed they are rather similar in appearance and personality. At the launch of the agency, "I figured I knew a lot about how the industry runs, and though I felt sure I could fill up my roster with existing thriller writers, I wanted to go out after new ones too."

Among the authors he now nurtures are Sarah Dunn, P.T. Deutermann, Chris Moore, Olivia Goldsmith (who came to him after *First Wives Club* and has since written that inside-publishing novel *The Bestseller*), Philip Rosenberg ("I've worked with him eight years on a big Mafia novel that's being submitted soon"), and James Webb, a former assistant secretary of defense who has made a considerable name as a novelist (*Fields of Fire* and now *The Emperor's General*).

Ellison has a list of only fifty to sixty clients ("This means that every book counts"), three-quarters of them fiction authors, an unusually high proportion. Generally he hears of potential new clients by word of mouth, "but if one of my assistants tells me to read something I'll read it, and call." What he's looking for, says Ellison, is "a voice—I couldn't care less about past successes or failures." He works very closely with the authors; "in fact I feel much closer to them editorially than I ever did while I was actually working as an editor." According to him, "80 percent of what I do is simply offering an anticipatory sense of the marketplace." He is ebullient about the turn his life has taken. "Finally, and it took ten years, agenting is becoming fun. You get to read great books, and I earn three times what I did in publishing. And when a novel really works, it sells all over the world: it's like a bank."

He is particularly well-connected for foreign sales, being affiliated as he is with Sanford Greenburger Associates, one of the premier international rights dealers, with whom he also shares offices. (The late Greenburger founded the firm in 1932 and was probably the first-ever foreign scout for United States publishers, as well as being an active seller of rights into the United States for foreign publishers, including the work of such notable writers as Albert Camus, Jean-Paul Sartre, Simone de Beauvoir, and the estate of Franz Kafka. Ellison describes Sanford Greenburger's Theresa Park, one of the firm's star agents, as "brilliant—she could be anything anywhere.")

As befits a former publisher who knows how they think and work, Ellison has a number of gripes with his customers. "I hate that eternal reserve for returns," he says. "Publishers should let it go after a year or eighteen months. And it makes the statements of net copies sold in their royalty forms a lie—those include returns, of course." He also hates the way that the two-tiered royalty system penalizes success, by offering a lower royalty on books sold at a higher discount. "That's not fair, and it's enraging."

"There should be licensing of agents—there's a lot of abuse in terms of greed and inappropriate behavior. And there are a lot of editors who give good lunch and are glib enough but have no knack with the pencil."

He finds that the overall quality of both editors and agents could be improved. "There should be licensing of agents—there's a lot of abuse in terms of greed and inappropriate behavior. And there are a lot of editors who give good lunch and are glib enough, but have no knack with the pencil. Yes, I'm aware of the corporate pressures and that they feel they have to please the financial officer rather than the editorial head, worshiping the deal itself rather than the written word that gave rise to it."

He warms to his theme. "There are too many trivial people doing pedestrian books. There are too many unethical things, people who don't call you back when they promise they will, lies on the size of printings." He sighs: "A sense of courtesy, a feeling that we're all partners in a common cause and should treat each other decently, that's dwindling in the industry, and I think it's a cause for dismay."

WHO: Nicholas Ellison, Inc.

WHERE: 55 Fifth Ave.
New York, NY 10003
212-206-6050; fax: 212-463-8718

WHAT: Fiction (especially thrillers), about 75 percent, some general nonfiction.

LIST: About fifty-five clients, including Nelson DeMille, James Webb, Olivia Goldsmith, Sarah Dunn, P.T. Deutermann, Chris Moore, Philip Rosenberg.

Lynn C. Franklin

Lynn C. Franklin Associates Ltd.

Lynn Franklin is one of the most internationally-minded of American agents—as a partner with Todd Siegal in Franklin & Siegal, an international scouting operation, and with her own literary agency in Lynn Franklin Associates. "Each one helps fertilize the other," she says.

Franklin, with a background in publishing and bookselling, is a dark-haired woman in her early fifties who looks considerably younger, and exudes an air of unshakable confidence and optimism. In 1993 she was reunited with a son she had placed for adoption in 1966 and, typically, threw herself into finding out everything she could about adoption, so that today, outside of her busy business life, she is a trustee of one of New York's premier adoption agencies, and is the author of a book, *May the Circle Be Unbroken: An Intimate Journey Into the Heart of Adoption,* published in 1998 by Harmony Books.

At Washington's American University, where she graduated with a B.A. in French in 1968, she worked in a local public library. After graduation she migrated briefly to San Francisco, where she worked in a European bookstore before taking a job at Sydney Kramer Books in Washington. From there she was invited to join the New York office of the

French publisher Hachette, and for six years beginning in 1969, worked in various departments, on promotion, catalogs, and finally direct marketing.

When she began to freelance, her interests almost at once became strongly international. Putting an ad for her services in London's *Bookseller* magazine, she heard from Felix Gluck, a London-based book packager, and made her first of over twenty annual visits to the Frankfurt International Book Fair, on his behalf, in 1976. While there, she met the people from Paul Hamlyn's enormously innovative London publishing/packaging operation Octopus, and worked for them for eight years, helping them to break, very successfully, into the United States market with Americanized titles.

It was a few years later that she began her scouting activities—seeking out potential American properties for translation and publication by foreign publishers—in earnest, having met Alain Stanke at the Montreal Book Fair and begun to scout for him in New York; that was when she began to meet some of those who later became colleagues in the scouting game, people like Maria Campbell and Christina McInerney. Eventually she moved on from Stanke and landed a job in 1978 as United States scout for the big German publisher Wilhelm Heyne Verlag, whom she and partner Todd Siegal still represent twenty years later. In 1981 she bought out the scouting interests of Paul Nathan in the United Kingdom and Scandinavia, and now represents some sixteen publishers worldwide. The scouting side is her busiest, employing eight people—there is even a special department for movies—while there are only two in her literary agency.

Compared to some agents, Franklin has only a comparatively small and select client list; there are about twenty-five active clients, producing perhaps ten books a year. It is mostly nonfiction, with an emphasis on biography and memoir, as well as titles in medicine, alternative health, and spirituality. She doesn't rule out fiction, but so far has done very little, because she has preferred to concentrate on nonfiction where she is sure of her strengths. "I'll probably hire someone to help me develop fiction as my agency grows."

Most of her clients come to her through referrals, though some arrive via over-the-transom submissions. "My very first sale came that way: a book on motivational speaking I sold to Berkley for very little." She wouldn't accept such an offer now, however; "You need big books to survive."

Among Franklin's best-known clients are the distinguished Russian writer Edward Radzinsky, whose *The Last Tsar* she sold six years ago to the late Jacqueline Kennedy Onassis at Doubleday, and which became a big best-seller for that house. Franklin met him through her extensive activities in Russia, where she was a pioneer Western agent when she first went there in 1988 at the suggestion of a Finnish client, noted editor Matti Snell.

> *"These days it's your job to persuade the publishers that there's an audience and that your author can reach it; all too often the marketing and publicity departments can't see the possibilities you know are there."*

"I wanted to help Russian writers find Western publishers, and at first I worked on a voluntary basis," she says. Then, as Communism retreated and entrepreneurial publishing began in Moscow, she began to sell rights to some Western authors there, eventually representing some twenty United States publishers and agents. She continued to make regular trips to Russia until two of her staffers, eager to try their hand in the new Eastern European market, went out there and with her blessing set up their own shop, taking over her existing clients.

For Radzinsky's book, Franklin negotiated personally with Mrs. Onassis, discussing editorial questions with her at regular intervals ("Yes, she really was an extraordinary editor").

Radzinsky has gone on to write a major new book about Stalin, based on many previously secret documents, which was published in 1996, and is now working on a book about the "mad monk" Rasputin.

Archbishop Desmond Tutu of South Africa is another celebrated client, met through a mutual friend, and Rafer Johnson, the gold medal decathlon winner at the 1960 Olympic Games, who had an inspirational memoir out in 1998, is another. Franklin also represented the son of a huge seller, Deepak Chopra: Gautama Chopra's first novel *Child of the Dawn,* in the form of a spiritual parable, had a first printing of 80,000 copies.

Some of the problems Franklin has with publishers are familiar from other agents, but she has some novel solutions. "With the seasonal lists, there's only a tiny window of opportunity with each list," she says. "The agent has to work very hard, and very closely with the publisher, to ensure the book doesn't get lost. And it's the agent's job to build some sort of reputation, or base, for the author, give publicity and marketing something to work with. I've even been known to tell clients to hire their own publicists to build themselves up before submitting their work for publication. These days it's your job to persuade the publisher there's an audience, and your author can reach it; all too often the marketing and publicity departments can't see the possibilities you know are there."

She goes on: "A lot of the job these days consists in educating clients about what to expect, what can and can't be done, and holding their hand through the whole laborious process. It takes longer to get paid than it used to, much longer to prepare and deliver contracts. And the problem of the vanishing editor is always with us."

One of the great rewards of life as an agent, she feels, is when she senses she can really make a vital contribution to a worthy project that otherwise might not get done. "For instance, I found Rafer Johnson a great collaborator in Philip Goldberg, and that made a tremendous difference."

WHO: Lynn C. Franklin Associates Ltd.

WHERE: 386 Park Avenue South (Ste. 1102)
New York, NY 10016
212-689-1842; fax: 212-213-0649
email: agency@fsainc.com

WHAT: Largely nonfiction list, including biography and memoir, alternative health, spirituality. Important international scouting interests (with Todd Siegal).

LIST: About twenty-five clients, producing ten books a year, including Edward Radzinsky, Desmond Tutu, Rafer Johnson.

Arnold and Elise Goodman

Goodman Associates

Arnold Goodman came to agenting by an unusual route: the theater. One summer, while he was at Yale, his mother was invited by a close friend of Gertrude Lawrence to see her in *The King and I,* and young Goodman tagged along. There he met Lawrence's lawyer, who discovered that the young freshman had a passion for the theater and arranged for him to get work in the box office of a summer theater near Boston. "I fell in love with it, and worked for several years in summer theater," he says with a reminiscent gleam. A spell in the army followed, then law school, supported by the G.I. Bill, before Goodman was able to take a job with an entertainment law firm that had many starry clients. In 1962 he was hired away by the Ashley Famous agency, which had a number of high-powered agents with both literary and dramatic clients—people of the level of Audrey Wood, Kay Brown, and Phyllis Jackson. Goodman became the house lawyer, writing and handling their contracts for seven years, but gradually found himself becoming more agent than lawyer, more and more involved with writers rather than show business folk, "and more interested in them too—more than in the legal stuff and the contracts."

Goodman is a silver-haired man with a decisive, somewhat sardonic manner. The offices of Goodman Associates are in a spacious Upper West Side Manhattan apartment that he shares with Elise (though she does not appear for the interview). "Everyone says it's a bad idea to work with your wife, but in fact it's worked out fine," he says. He acknowledges that there were some "tough times" in the early days of the agency, deciding who did what, but they have now worked out a system whereby they consult on all decisions. Each has his or her own client list, but Arnold, as befits his past, does all the negotiating and works out all the contracts.

From the start they worked in their apartment, with their first offices in what had been the two maids' rooms, later cluttered with kids' bikes leaning against the walls. "The plan was to stay a couple of years, then find an office," says Goodman with a shrug. "But as you see, we're still here"—though the office is now much more spacious, the old dining room an elegantly furnished conference room.

For the agency, the moment of truth had come in 1975, when Arnold, because of his many theatrical clients and the management side of his career, was faced with a stern choice: if he wanted to continue to work with show business clients he would have to transplant himself to the West Coast. "But I'm a New Yorker born and bred, so I decided to stay here and become purely a literary agent. New York was the center of the publishing business, after all."

His first client, he recalls, was sent by his aunt, and delivered two piles of manuscript, each the size of a phone book, which turned out to be a novel called *One Smart Indian* by Robert Seidman, for which they found a publisher in Putnam. Goodman went to call on publishers, lunched with editors, excavated the slush pile; when he had an idea for a book he looked for a writer to execute it. "We've always been able to make a living on books that we're interested in." Elise is an enthusiastic and skillful cook ("I just eat it, and wash the pots"), and her interest brought in a number of food writers and their books.

For a time the Goodmans were *the* American agents for a sudden invasion of highly talented Australian writers. As Arnold remembers it, they had some time to kill at the Frankfurt Book Fair sometime around the mid-1980s, wandered beyond the British and American stands where they spent most of their time, and went into the Australian booth area. "They were lovely people, but they didn't have a clue about the New York scene. They were doing things like sending romances to Knopf." He took a book an Australian publisher offered, sold it for $25,000 to an American house, "and word went round like a bush fire." After a time they found themselves dealing with the handful of Australian agents too, and soon picked up United States representation for an impressive Australian fiction list: the likes of Tim Winton, Kate Grenville, Elizabeth Jolley, and, for a while, Thea Astley.

Still, despite that literary outpouring, these days the balance at the Goodman agency is decidedly toward nonfiction, by a margin of about 70 percent nonfiction to 30 percent fiction. "It's so hard to find good fiction, then so hard to sell it," Goodman says.

Their most successful project ever, and one that could all by itself make the agency one of the more profitable ones, is the series that began with *What to Expect When You're Expecting,* an encyclopedic guide to pregnancy written in a winning, down-to-earth style by a neighboring Upper West Side family, the Eisenbergs: Mother Arlene, and daughters Heidi and Sandee. This book has now sold more than 7 million copies for Workman Publishing since it first appeared in 1984, and has had translations into more than thirty languages. Various sequels and spin-offs follow the growing baby year-by-year; all have enjoyed stellar sales—over 15 million copies worldwide and continuing to build. It is the biggest phenomenon of its kind since Dr. Spock's baby bible of the 1950s and 1960s "It's an industry," explains Goodman.

Another major and highly profitable undertaking is the series of vegetarian cookbooks published under the rubric of the Moosewood Restaurant in Ithaca, N.Y. It was the Goodmans' daughter Emily, home from freshman year at college, who brought them the news of "a great new vegetarian cookbook." It had been self-published initially, then sold to California's Ten Speed Press. When the Moosewood people decided they wanted a larger house and more exposure they sent out letters to more than thirty possible agents seeking representation. "We went right up to Ithaca to see them, and they hired us," says Goodman. Following some protracted litigation to retrieve the Moosewood name, the restaurant and its writers have created six new books. The next two will be at Clarkson Potter, at Crown, for over seven figures.

"These days it's your job to persuade the publishers that there's an audience and that your author can reach it; all too often the marketing and publicity departments can't see the possibilities you know are there."

Goodman finds that he and Elise are now "slowing down, taking on new projects more carefully, doing more servicing of our ongoing series, less acquiring." While they used to go to writers' conferences and book shows, they seldom do so any longer. Still, despite the slowdown, he notes with satisfaction that their most recent year has been the most prosperous ever—though he also remarks that the effort that goes into building up such a situation "takes a long time to pay off."

He is not sanguine about recent changes he has seen in the book business. "The various publishers used to have identities; stamped on them by the heads of the company. Now they're all homogenized, Disneyfied—that's why Peter Workman is so unusual, because he's not. We often find we have to go further and further afield to get things we really believe in published. We'll work with the smaller publishers when we have to, but it takes an eternity to get anything read, and there's much less money in it." But they continue to keep their eyes open for "more unusual, offbeat things." A book called *Riddle of the Ice* by Myron Arms, recently discovered in the slush pile, became a lead title for Doubleday's Anchor Books.

He also worries about "more layers of bureaucracy. They seem to need six signatures for a check. And the marketing department has an inordinate influence. I lost a sale not long ago because it was felt that publicity *might* not be able to get the author on 'Oprah'! And I feel that the big bookstore chains are dictating too much of what gets published. That's one of the things we're up against." But it's not the kind of worry that can make much of a dent on an operation fuelled by two such blockbusters as *Expecting* and *Moosewood*.

WHO: Goodman Associates
Arnold Goodman, Elise Goodman

WHERE: 500 West End Ave.
New York, NY 10024
212-873-4806

WHAT: General fiction and nonfiction, emphasis on practical advice; about 70 percent nonfiction, including cookbooks.

LIST: About sixty active clients, including Arlene, Heidi, and Sandee Eisenberg, Moosewood.

Joy Harris

Joy Harris Literary Agency

Long associated in the book world with agent
Robert Lantz (and in fact at the time of the interview the name on the door to her lower Fifth
Avenue office was still the Lantz-Harris Literary
Agency), Joy Harris is now the mistress of her own
domain. Looking out from behind stylish glasses,
she seems rather like a sixties folk singer on the
Joan Baez model, with dark hair and a warm, lively manner.

With a Ph.D. in psychology, she taught emotionally handicapped children in New York public
schools for a while. In the summer of 1978 she
shared a house with a group of writers and found
she loved what they did. Following a move to
California, she landed a job at a bookstore as one
way of getting closer to them. Returning to New
York a year later, she entered a program at Columbia
University for women changing careers. "I knew I
wanted to work with writers, and was determined to
find a way."

As part of the Columbia program, Harris did a
brief internship with agent Knox Burger. "It was
thrilling. He loaded me down with manuscripts,
including *Gorky Park*, and wanted to hear what I
thought about them. I did everything from filing

papers and answering query letters to writing reports on manu-scripts. I can't tell you how exciting it was to be immersed in the world of the written word." That brief internship led to a part-time job with the late agent Connie Clausen. "She was so pas-sionate and funny. It was a great first-paying-job in agenting." That was followed by an introduction to agent Robert Lantz, whose clients included Leonard Bernstein.

Harris's mother, who worked for Bernstein, had suggested her daughter go see Lantz about the possibility of a full-time job. " 'He probably won't offer you a job, but maybe he'll have some advice for you,' " she said. "Luckily for me, he had advice, and a job, too. Bobby wanted someone who was not a secretary, was not involved in show business. He wanted me to work on the book side. It was an invaluable learning experience. He'd let me take on as much as I could handle, including permission requests, selling foreign rights and, of course, extensive client contact."

The Lantz Office handled some remarkable clients, includ-ing Tommy Thompson, Shana Alexander, Lillian Hellman, and the estates of Romain Gary, Dashiell Hammett, and Carson McCullers. Lantz was also known for his representation of peo-ple from the show business world, and when stars like Elizabeth Taylor, Bette Davis, and Michael Jackson decided to write books, they turned to the agency. "It was trial by fire in the early days of the celebrity autobiography," Harris says.

While Harris looked after Lanz's clients, she also began to build a list of her own. "I got to know editors who would refer people to me, so would other writers. It just spreads outward in circles, like ripples on a pond." She also became associated with the M.F.A. program at the University of California at Irvine. It was an exciting time in that program's history, and several of the writers became her clients, including Jay Gummerman, Whitney Otto, Louis Jones. Biographer Lawrence Leamer (*The Kennedy Men, The Kennedy Women*) and Mark Singer also joined at this time.

Until 1990 she was a salaried employee, then became a partner in the newly formed Lantz-Harris Literary Agency. Lantz, who continued to run the Lantz Office for directors, playwrights, and screenwriters, could now retire from the book side whenever he wanted, "and I would take over the entire literary agency." That happened in 1993, "a smooth transition. I couldn't have been more fortunate."

"I'm having to become the shadow publisher, which means following up on every detail during the publishing process. It's endlessly time-consuming. I find myself so preoccupied with worry over the possibility of details falling through the cracks that I'm not having nearly as much fun as I used to."

Harris has about one hundred clients, roughly 60 percent of them in nonfiction, though she doesn't generally give them ideas. "Most of them generate their own, and I help talk them through to a good proposal." Her taste in nonfiction is eclectic, ranging from serious biography to popular culture. "If a writer is good enough, he or she can interest me in a subject I didn't think I was interested in," an example: space exploration. So, naturally Jeffrey Kluger came to her with a proposal on the ill-fated Apollo 13 mission. "This also happened to be a time when the publishing industry had no interest in the space program. Jeff had been told by other agents he saw that that they didn't think they could sell his book. I felt he was such a good writer that if he could write a great proposal I could sell it. It was Jeff's idea to approach Jim Lovell, the commander of Apollo 13, who agreed to a collaboration." The book that resulted was a very successful hardcover, and later became the basis of the hit Ron Howard movie. It's not always the writing that allures Harris. "

It may not be brilliant, but if the emotional impact, or the enthusiasm, or the knowledge, is really compelling, you have to do it."

In many ways she feels that better publishing is being done today because of the greater pressure, but at a cost. "Relationships are tougher; there used to be more of a sense of congeniality, but now everyone is feeling the pressure to perform, and get media attention." There's too much inefficiency in publishing houses, she thinks. "I sometimes feel that with all the following up I have to do I'm doing ten jobs. It's a question of details—flap copy, catalog copy, sudden changes being made that I'm not convinced will work. I'm having to become the shadow publisher, which means following up on every detail during the publishing process. It's endless and endlessly time-consuming. I find myself so preoccupied with worry over the possibility of details falling through the cracks that I'm not having nearly as much fun as I once did. I know I'm not alone in feeling this way."

Editors "went into publishing for a different reason than thinking about margins, and I think a lot of them are having a hard time. If you take away, or discount, people's instincts and passions, then what are they doing? Why are they there? There's more second-guessing of them being done than ever, and not just by one or two people. There are many decisions that can't be made through groups or majority votes. It's okay to have editors who know how to sell a book, but that shouldn't be their only qualification. It's always been easier to say no than yes, but now it's *too* easy. What I find upsetting is that I once believed all books worth publishing would find a home. I no longer think that's true."

Harris has found she is going more often to small publishers with worthy books rejected elsewhere, but "I always worry about their distribution." These days, with big distributors like Publishers Group West and National Book Network becoming more effective, those worries are somewhat lessened, and she feels the situation is likely to improve further as big publishers give up on some of the smaller books. She looks for long-term investment in her authors from publishers, "but given the circumstances today, I think we have to be realistic and accept that for many authors this is no longer a fair expectation."

The agency reads everything that is submitted, and "Occasionally, I find a Judy Mercer (author of *Fast Forward* and *Doubletake*), and that makes it all worthwhile."

WHO: Joy Harris Literary Agency

WHERE: 156 Fifth Ave.
New York, NY 10010
212-924-6269; fax: 212-924-6609

WHAT: General nonfiction (about 60 percent) and fiction.

LIST: About one hundred clients, including Whitney Otto, Louis Jones, Lawrence Leamer, Mark Singer, Jeffrey Kluger, Judy Mercer.

Member of AAR

Fred Hill

Frederick Hill Associates

Everyone in publishing knows Fred Hill. With more than thirty-five years in the business, much of it in highly visible areas like sales, marketing, and advertising, with extensive experience overseas, and now with nearly twenty years of increasingly successful agenting behind him, he is as familiar a figure at the Frankfurt Book Fair as at one of the book parties on either coast (he works out of San Francisco) he loves to attend. And people are glad to see him, because the bulky, genial man with the lived-in face, the ready chuckle, the love of gossip, and the endless flow of entertaining stories, is downright good company.

Interviewed in a trendy coffee shop in the Flatiron district of New York, on one of his frequent trips to the city to see publishers and friends (often the same thing), he is full of rollicking stories of his early days in the business that for the purposes of an interview have to be heavily curtailed to let the salient facts shine through.

Briefly, then, he was born in Philadelphia, went to Brown University, thence to the Army, and then, as young men often did in those days—the late 1950s—messed around for a time while deciding what he wanted to do with his life. After his Army discharge, which he contrived to have happen in Spain, he stayed there for a while, working as a stringer for UPI, teaching English, and attending the University of Madrid, before returning to the States in 1961 with a vague idea that he might go into publishing—"not necessarily as an editor." Hired by the Random House college division, he was offered a job as a "field editor," which turned out to mean a sales job, with a territory that included colleges from Princeton to Brown but excluded New York. Hill stuck it out for a year, found he hated it, then went to Denhard & Stewart, one of the top publisher advertising agencies, handling major trade publishers. There he wrote copy for the top publishing houses and began to become familiar with the book world and its terms. "I went to all the sales conferences, got to know everyone." This led to the offer of a job as sales director at Macmillan, but new management, in the person of one Raymond Hagel, came aboard and it became an unhappy place to be. Hill's next leap was to Little, Brown, who was looking for a resident sales rep in the West ("It all seemed very collegial, and men in those days made their way to the top of publishing houses by way of jobs in sales"). Typically, he stayed at the luxurious and exotic Chateau Marmont in Los Angeles while looking for somewhere to live. This period—not the hotel stay—lasted five years, during which Time Life bought the publisher, and, as it bought a number of foreign imprints too, the international arena began to open up.

Hill, with his early European experience, was summoned back to Boston (Little, Brown headquarters) to develop an international sales department. He went to the Frankfurt Book Fair for the first time in 1969, the early days of foreign sales for United States properties. "Time had brought its foreign publishers, thinking there would be synergy. That didn't work, of course, but I loved the international arena, seeing how things were done elsewhere, other styles of doing business." He got to know significant European publishers like Andre Laffont, Andre Deutsch, and George Weidenfeld, links that were to stand him in good stead later. The international side grew and prospered, but Little, Brown decided to move Hill into another job, and made him marketing director. This increased his knowledge of books and authors, but he decided that after ten years he wanted to make a major life change. "I went to France and sat on a mountain to meditate." The result? He moved to San Francisco and joined the fledgling publishing arm of the conservationist Sierra Club as managing director, working with Jon Beckmann as editorial director. This was a lively time for the club, which published Eliot Porter's magnificent photo books, later done in paperback by Ian Ballantine, and "I had a lot of fun there for five years, but in the end I found it too specialized."

Meanwhile, however, he had found that San Francisco was rich in writers, and was, to put it mildly, under-agented. "I decided I could do it," and he launched his agency in 1979. His first office was a fifth-floor walk-up, and he trolled for clients among local newspaper people. Old friends like the late veteran West Coast editor William Abrahams would suggest him to writers, who in turn would send other writers. "But it was pretty thin for the first couple of years. In those days I would have sold anything that anyone would buy." But although it was five years before he broke even, two writers who were to lay the foundation for the agency's very considerable later fortunes were enrolled almost from the start. One was Richard North Patterson, ace writer of legal thrillers, sent to him by Robert Manning at the *Atlantic Monthly;* Patterson had published a short story in the magazine and was looking for an agent. The other was *San Francisco Chronicle* reporter Randy Shilts, whose bestselling success with *And the Band Played On,* the first major book to tell the whole AIDS story, made Hill into an agent with visibility at last. He is still bitter, however, about the resistance many publishers expressed toward the book, and the many turndowns he and Shilts suffered through before Michael Denneny at St. Martin's Press took it on. Even then the advance was so comparatively small that it was a struggle for years to get more to keep Shilts going through the years it took to write the book. In the end the author succumbed to AIDS himself.

Cookbooks are another significant part of Hill's offerings, which he reckons are currently divided about equally between fiction and nonfiction. He himself has an instinct, he feels, for commercial fiction, and he is very specific about what works and what doesn't. He looks first of all for "authority, for a hint of something I haven't seen before, a sense of personality that sets the work apart."

"I love being in a business where you can constantly meet people you would like even if they were in some other business."

The more literary side of the agency is represented by his partner Bonnie Nadell, who worked in subsidiary rights at Simon & Schuster, who came out and joined him a few years into the agency, and who has now been there fifteen years; she runs Hill's Los Angeles office. "She adds a dimension, and between us I think we cover the bases. She knows the younger editors, who will be the senior people in the next decade; I sometimes feel most of the people I grew up in the business with are dead or retired. It was Bonnie who discovered David Foster Wallace when he was only twenty-four. She has this knack for very young and very gifted literary people." Nadell has an interest in the agency, and while Hill threatens never to retire, he says she will inevitably take over more and more of the day-to-day running of it.

There's also an assistant, Irene Moore, who joined five years ago, works for both the partners, and is beginning to do things on her own, "making audio deals." It is she who will talk, if necessary, to people who call offering to send in material. Yes, Hill and Nadell do look at it, though they urge letters or proposals first.

Hill is expansive about the pleasures of agenting. "I love the visibility, I love being in a business where you constantly meet people you would like even if they were in some other business. I don't just take on books and authors to pump up the volume. I think vertically, not horizontally, and I don't take on clients just to lengthen the list. I just want to make very good sales on a few books. It's so much a matter of chemistry, finding the right authors to go with the right editors; perhaps some alchemy too," he grins. He seems immune to the changes in the business in recent years that most agents note so dourly. "I don't see much difference from before. Sure, there's some attrition. I've lost a lot of old friends, but I make a point to keep meeting new people. And I'm convinced that if you have a really good book you'll sell it."

WHO: Frederick Hill Associates
Fred Hill, Bonnie Nadell

WHERE: 1842 Union St.
San Francisco, CA 94123
415-921-2910; fax: 415-921-2802

WHAT: General fiction and nonfiction, about 50-50, with some concentration on thrillers, cookbooks, some literary fiction.

LIST: About one hundred active clients, including Richard North Patterson, David Foster Wallace, Katherine Neville, Randy Shilts, John Mandel, David Hunt, Mark Childress, Antonia Nelson, Nicole Mones.

Barney Karpfinger

The Karpfinger Agency

Karpfinger is a carefully groomed man whose offices, recently shaped out of the ground floor and basement of a handsome Chelsea townhouse, are among the most elegant in the city. He is almost a Zen idea of an agent—quiet, affable, unassuming, utterly laid back—though in fact he has seen his share of Sturm und Drang, and it is only comparatively recently that he has begun enjoying the fruits of success.

He began in publishing after graduating from Columbia and working his way through school as a paralegal, but, like so many agents, for a long time couldn't get the kind of work—editing—that he had hoped for. In 1977 he took a job as assistant to the rights director at Hawthorn, and when his boss quit and Karpfinger had in effect taken on her job and improved the revenue, he asked for the title too. He didn't get it, and left. But with his experience he secured a job running the contracts department at Dutton. "It was a great time to be there. Henry Robbins was the editor-in-chief, they were about to publish *Garp* and Fran Lebowitz's first book, and it was all very exciting." He expanded his reach into permissions and royalties, "but it all seemed to be getting further and further away from where I wanted to be, which was books and editorial."

Someone suggested to him that an agent could combine the kinds of things he wanted to do, so in 1979 Karpfinger took a job as assistant to literary agent John Schaffner. "I took a better than 50 percent cut in salary to do it, but it turned out to be the smartest thing I ever did." The agency, he soon discovered, was in a state of considerable disarray. "I began to fix it up and to take on some of my own clients, then got a 33 percent partnership. I had expected to take the agency over on Schaffner's retirement, but it turned out his son wanted to go into the business, so that was that." He sold back his share, and went to work for Aaron Priest at his eponymous agency. "I did my own list there, handled foreign rights—I learned a great deal from Aaron." But their styles were too different. "I was more laid back, and I figured it wasn't working."

So in early 1984 Karpfinger went off on his own, taking his clients with him. "I had an entrepreneurial family background, and I'd worked it out that I had income to survive for a year." In the meantime he had taken on Jonathan Kellerman (who turned out eventually to be a huge success, but was, says Karpfinger, a hard sell at first), Aaron Elkins, and some promising cookbook authors. He sublet a tiny space on 48th Street, with a small but comfortable office, and a huge terrace with a view of St. Patrick's Cathedral, "and there was a great receptionist." He worked there with increasing success for three years, and took on an assistant, before his landlord went bankrupt, necessitating a sudden move.

After his move into another building, things began to improve even further. Kellerman's first novel did very well in paperback, and his career began to take off. Meanwhile Karpfinger took on some *New York Times* writers, Samuel G. Freedman and Michael Winerip, a professional cookbook author, Jean Anderson (of Doubleday Cookbook fame), and began to do some literary fiction by the likes of David Carkeet,

Bill Morris, and William Hallberg. More commercial thriller writers came aboard, including Andrew Klavan, Kellerman's wife Faye, and John T. Lescroart.

After looking for several years for a place where he could both live and work, Karpfinger finally found and moved into his Chelsea house in 1993. He now has three key associates: Olivia Blumer, whom he hired away from her job as vice president and rights director at Warner, and who naturally handles all foreign rights and brings in her own clients; Joe Gramm, who is his assistant and does author accounts; and Jennifer Unter, who handles contracts, first serial rights, and audio.

The agency's list is small, thirty to thirty-five, divided about equally between fiction and nonfiction (there are several cookbook authors), though fiction brings in considerably more than half the revenue. Most new clients come in by recommendation from existing clients or editors, though "every now and again something comes up in the slush." Everything gets at least looked at, with Karpfinger himself glancing at entries from time to time. "Most of it is quite well written," he says. "It's the concepts, the idea that this or that could be a book, that are usually at fault."

"Publishing houses are far less willing than they used to be to take leaps of faith. I worry that they're not investing in authors in small ways, keeping faith with them through the quiet times."

He finds that it is new authors of nonfiction who need the most help. "A really good proposal is an unusual form, and I work very hard with clients to get it just right." He rarely does line editing: "It's more conceptual. I try to figure out where the author wants to be going; sometimes I can help, sometimes not." Whether or not they need help, he talks to his authors a lot, keeps in close touch.

He has mixed feelings about current editorial standards at publishing houses. "There are some editors around now who are better and more attentive than editors have ever been; there are also a number who are very lazy and ill-informed. And of course publishing houses are far less willing than they used to be to take leaps of faith. I worry that they're not investing in authors in small ways, keeping faith with them through the quiet times." Like most agents, he finds payments and royalty statements are later than they used to be; "publishers are trying to hang on to the money as long as possible."

Karpfinger is a strong believer in an agent having a hand in as many details of a book's progress as possible. "Yes, I think an agent should be staying on top of things like jackets, and I write consultation on such things into my contracts." Anyone who has been in Karpfinger's offices should be perfectly willing to give him his way in terms of design.

WHO: The Karpfinger Agency
Barney Karpfinger, Olivia Blumer

WHERE: 357 West 20th St.
New York, NY 10011
212-691-2690

WHAT: General fiction and nonfiction, about 50-50, some stress on cookbooks.

LIST: About thirty-five active clients, including Jonathan Kellerman, Faye Kellerman, Jean Anderson, Aaron Elkins, Michael Winerip, Andrew Klavan, John T. Lescroart.

Harvey Klinger

Harvey Klinger, Inc.

Harvey Klinger began his literary life by trying to *get* an agent, not to be one. A genial, fast-talking, bushy-haired man with a mustache, he had started out as a would-be writer in the graduate school of The Writing Seminars at Johns Hopkins that had numbered among its alumni writers of the stature of John Barth and Russell Baker. He had originally planned to go to journalism school, went to Hopkins instead, found it pleasant, but had no idea at the end of it what he planned to do. Asked by the dean for his plans, he assumed he would either write the Great American Novel or go to New York and try to get into publishing.

The latter turned out to be his course, and he entered Doubleday's celebrated training course, but lasted only four months. "It seemed like too bureaucratic an environment." Then he heard that the late agent Jay Garon, later to become famous as John Grisham's representative, but then subsisting mostly on gothic novels, needed an assistant, and went there. "I worked for Jay for eighteen months and learned how *not* to do it," he laughs. "He shoveled out loads of stuff hoping some of it would stick, and had some of his poor romance writers working their fingers to the bone."

In 1975 he met a woman who worked as a celebrity publicist, and who wanted an associate to expand her agency. They worked together for two years, with Klinger drawing a salary plus small commissions, but "it wasn't working financially," and he decided to go off on his own—though they continued to share offices until 1990. The offices Klinger's agency now occupies are in a high-rise apartment building on Eighth Avenue, just west of the theater district.

He acknowledges that getting incorporated, which he did in 1979, was "terrifying," but he had a couple of aces up his sleeve. Author Terry Kline wanted to join him though he had a five-year contract with Garon (on which the agent insisted), and in order to do so he had to write under another name. Then there was Barbara Wood, a prolific writer who had already written seven novels without selling anything. She submitted *Hounds and Jackals* to Ballantine, asked them about an agent, and they steered her to Klinger. He swiftly sold three of her books in his first six months, and was off and running, though he acknowledges it was a couple more years before he felt sure he would make it. (Wood, meanwhile, has become a huge seller in Germany, where her titles have sold over 7 million copies.)

One of the things that helped, beyond the fact that "there weren't nearly so many agents then," was that the late seventies and early eighties was the big time for paperback sales. "You could have a $20,000 advance, then turn around and make a $400,000 paperback sale. The paperback houses mostly functioned independently then, so you didn't have all the hard-soft deals. Eventually, I'm afraid, the paperback houses wised up to the fact that the hardcover houses had come to depend on big paperback payments, and wouldn't make any effort to sell the book themselves and build a market."

As the agency grew so did the number of submissions, though virtually all the clients are taken on through referrals. "I can count on one hand the writers who came out of the slush pile." He now has two assistants to read it all, and also an associate, in Laurie Liss, who has made something of a shtick out of discovering unlikely successes in material deemed hopeless by the critics. Liss joined him after unearthing Robert James Waller (*Bridges of Madison County*) for Aaron Priest, and going on to find the self-published (in Utah) *Christmas Box* and its successors by Richard Paul Evans, which have made a mint of money. "Laurie is an associate, not a partner, but she is *very* well compensated," Klinger says. They work as a team, though their tastes differ ("I would never have taken on Waller").

"There are still houses where you have some of the old-line, committed editors, but they're up against behemoths in sales and marketing. On the other hand, people would sign up books twenty years ago where sales didn't have a clue, so perhaps the changes aren't altogether a bad thing."

Klinger estimates he has about one hundred authors in the stable, with about a third of them producing books in any given year. They are just about evenly balanced between fiction and nonfiction, "though it could tip one way or the other from year to year." In nonfiction, publishers are always looking for authors with the right credentials—a Harvard degree, a perfect shrink. He works very closely with authors to get their proposals into shape; "that's the creative side, what gets me going." Once he feels something is in top shape for submission, "I'm not concerned with where or how it's going to sell. I *know* it will." Barbara De Angelis, for instance, came recommended by an attorney, but having read her original proposal for *How to Make Love All the Time,* he asked if she was willing to work with him on it. He worked it over three times before selling it, and De Angelis has gone on to a notable career.

Klinger takes great pleasure in literary as well as commercial successes. Examples: Terry Kay, who had been with him for sixteen years and whose *To Dance with the White Dog* he couldn't place ("They all said the same thing: 'Love the writing, but how can we sell it?' ") until a small Southern publisher, Atlanta's Peachtree, took it, "and we made a fortune." Then there's Brian Morton, whose quietly elegant and touching *Starting Out in the Evening* made a critical stir and a decent paperback sale, but about whom Klinger exults as if he were a gold mine.

In nonfiction, he prefers subjects such as self-help psychology, wellness, and science. "I like to feel I'm learning something, and if I am, the readers are too. I like good biographies, but they're awfully difficult to do now: the problem of finding a new subject, then getting the inevitable extensions because it always takes longer than the author thinks." His list is "a reflection of the books I like to read—if I don't want to read it, I don't want to sell it." On fiction, "I'm always thinking of plots, but most novelists don't want you to think up things for them. My creative writing now is restricted to letters."

On the business today, "the more things change, the more they stay the same. Consolidation has meant a loss of suppliers; there are now only twenty wholesalers buying paperbacks instead of two hundred, and there used to be a lot more places to take a manuscript. There are still houses where you have some of the old-line, committed editors, but they're up against behemoths in sales and marketing. On the other hand, people would sign up books twenty years ago when sales didn't have a clue, so perhaps the changes aren't altogether a bad thing. You want to have your books sold, after all."

WHO: Harvey Klinger, Inc.
Harvey Klinger, Laurie Liss

WHERE: 301 West 53rd St.
New York, NY 10019
212-581-7068; fax: 212-315-3823
email: klingerinc@aol.com

WHAT: General nonfiction and fiction, balanced about evenly.

LIST: About one hundred clients producing about thirty books a year, including Barbara Wood, Terry Kline, Richard Paul Evans, Barbara De Angelis, Terry Kay, Brian Morton.

Member of AAR

Peter Lampack

Peter Lampack Agency, Inc.

Peter Lampack seems to be an agent to whom things have come comparatively easily. With relatives who were prepared to help him on his way, with an early client who turned out to be one of today's brand-name best-selling authors, and with what appears to be a calm, unruffled temperament, it is tempting to describe his career in terms of an agent born with the traditional silver spoon. Naturally, he hasn't always seen it quite that way.

A small-boned, neatly dressed man in his fifties with a husky voice and an instantly authoritative air like that of a good lawyer or accountant, he begins by saying that he "went through the mailroom, like everyone," at his first place of employment, the big William Morris agency. Coming out of college at twenty-one with no ambition to speak of, he was, he says, "lucky if I was able to find my way to the office in the morning." But since he had an uncle who was a published writer, he landed the Morris job, working at first as the first assistant to David Geffen, who later went on to bigger things in Hollywood—but who also, according to Lampack, went the mailroom route on his own way up. "I thought I'd be able to get an overview of the whole entertainment industry," says Lampack, and in fact he spent his ten years at Morris working mostly for the television and film divisions in turn. "I was involved with some books too, and with the play department."

Then at age thirty-two, in 1977, he was offered stock in the company, "and I knew if I accepted it I'd never be able to afford to leave. I had a wife and a son, and the temptation was strong, but I felt I didn't want to tie myself for life to my first job. When I told them I thought I'd have to leave they gave me a month to change my mind. It was tough; it wasn't that I was underpaid or underappreciated, and I liked the people—I thought they had basic decency and real integrity. I just didn't want to be hemmed in." So with considerable trepidation he went off on his own—but not without taking some clients, with permission, with him. These included Jeffrey Konvitz, whose paperback rights for *The Sentinel* had been sold for $300,000, and Clive Cussler, whose first best-seller, *Raise the Titanic* (yes, even then it was a name that could sell books) was published by Viking, sold to Bantam for paperback for $800,000 and to Lord Lew Grade of ITV in Britain for $500,000. As a television agent Lampack had also worked with producer Ed Spielman, the creator of the very popular Kung Fu series and had packaged some movies.

So he was not without resources when he became the Peter Lampack Agency, Inc. Further good fortune: his father-in-law owned interests in some clothing manufacturing companies with Manhattan offices, so he was able to move right into a little interior office without a window in one of them. "You had to go through racks of suits to get there." Lampack says he was scared to death for the first five years, though he amends this to say "I was emotionally scared for a good while, but I think that intellectually I felt secure sooner than that." He had a full-time assistant from the start (he now has three), and later moved to his present landmark office building on Fifth Avenue, where he occupies a bright, sleek set of offices on the sixteenth floor.

He insists, however, that "I always lived below my income, and worked very carefully. If you select the right kinds of writers, and progress with them, they will create more than enough income. It was never just the numbers game with me in terms of the size of the list." He says he has no more than thirty active clients, "and if you have too many you're just throwing darts at random, you can't really know what will work."

Although most agents have perforce to throw darts in this way, Lampack seems convinced he can tell well in advance what will work and what won't. His clients usually come to him by referral, from other authors, attorneys, friends—and one of his requirements is that they not be rivals within a genre: "I prefer not to have those kinds of conflicts." As a result his list represents what he calls "a large canvas," with a number of stars in different formats. There is Cussler for big-budget mainstream adventure fiction, South Africa's austere J.M. Coetzee for literary fiction, Gerry Spence for highly successful books on the lawyerly life, Martha Grimes as an ace mystery writer. Other authors on his list include Doris Mortman, Fred Mustard Stewart, Warren Adler, and Judith Kelman.

Lampack's list greatly favors fiction over nonfiction, probably by 75 percent-25 percent, and he says he still takes on new people occasionally, "if they have credentials, or a manuscript that's really good." He's deeply involved in the editing process: "Most manuscripts get a great deal of editing here; that's required these days to stay competitive."

Rather unusually, Lampack does not consider today's marketplace a tougher one than when he began. "Change is perpetual, and you have to adjust," he says. If you have a list of "unique" writers, the publishers need you. "Editors always return my calls." Certainly, he has had problems. "I sold too many authors at one time to one house, and several of them were dispossessed when there was a change of regime. I won't do that again." His pet peeve is that the larger houses have become so big "they need a huge legal and contractual bureaucracy to function, and these have grown far beyond what they should be. They therefore have to justify themselves to their management by making the whole process as laborious as possible." And he talks of one contract, just concluded, that took over a year to sign, and notes that "six months from agreement to contract is normal now."

"The mid-list editor is being washed out just like the mid-list author. The publishers don't emphasize editorial skills anymore, they ask the editors only to acquire manuscripts that can then go into the production process as quickly and cheaply as possible."

He observes that publishers benefit from this, as banks do, in having extended use of the money promised, and owed, to the author as a "float," and by keeping authors on tenterhooks as they work on their books. But it is not unique to publishing, says Lampack: "It's often the same way in the movies." He's not concerned about what some agents see as the dwindling number of imprints able to bid competitively on authors' work as the publishers expand. "I'm more afraid of their corporate owners handing down financial budgets they have to keep within, and then the editors will censor themselves to the point where they'll only do what they think of as sure things. I'm worried about the impact that's likely to have on the culture."

On that same level of the book culture, he is concerned about the declining role of the editor. "The mid-list editor is being washed out just like the mid-list author. The publishers don't emphasize editorial skills any more, they ask the editors only to acquire manuscripts that can then go into the production process as quickly and cheaply as possible." As a result, the burden of supplying publishable work now falls on the agents. "We don't get paid for it, and we don't really have time for it, but we have to do it."

Lampack recently signed a new deal for star author Cussler, with Simon & Schuster trade chief Jack Romanos, whereby a new series of books spun out from the Dirk Pitt series, which Cussler will supervise rather than write (in much the same way as some of Tom Clancy's series works), and in which payment will be made largely as a proportion of the profits the books make, after a comparatively low down payment in the form of an advance. It has been compared to a somewhat similar deal the same house (acting through Scribner) recently concluded with Stephen King after King split with Viking, his publisher of many years. In fact, says Lampack, Cussler's deal was in the making earlier, though King's was actually signed first. Do such arrangements represent a new way for big-money deals with top authors to be worked out? "They'll work only if they work out for the author," Lampack decides. "I think King is at some risk since he will personally author his books under this kind of deal. With Clive, it's more his co-workers who might stand to lose if the books don't work out as hoped." But naturally, with Lampack's self-confidence, he expects they will—and in any case his author is unlikely to suffer.

WHO: Peter Lampack Agency, Inc.

WHERE: 551 Fifth Ave. (Ste. 1613)
New York, NY 10176
212-687-9106; fax: 212-687-9109
email: renbopla@aol.com

WHAT: General fiction (about 75 percent) and nonfiction, representing authors in diverse fictional genres.

LIST: About thirty active clients, including Clive Cussler, Jeffrey Konvitz, J.M. Coetzee, Gerry Spence, Martha Grimes, Fred Mustard Stewart, Warren Adler, Doris Mortman, Judith Kelman.

Michael Larsen and Elizabeth Pomada

Michael Larsen/Elizabeth Pomada

There are not many husband-and-wife teams in agenting, and this San Francisco-based team is unusual in several ways. First is their appearance: Larsen is small and compact, hard-driving and fast-talking, a salesman if ever there was one, but with a refreshing leavening of wit; Pomada is large, placid and seemingly laid-back, though certainly not without enthusiasm. They started in 1972, and theirs is the longest-lived agency in Northern California. They seem omnipresent; they are constantly turning up on publishers' doorsteps pushing their authors and titles. They are both published authors, and continue to produce books, apart and together. And, as might be expected, they are regulars on the writers' conference circuit, lecturing, appearing on panels with some regularity, and always with an eye open for new clients.

Both came out of the promotional side of publishing, and a concern with—and knack for—promotion remains with them. Virtually alone among agents, they have a glossy four-page brochure about their agency, called *How To Make Yourself Irresistible to Any Agent or Publisher,* full of good advice about the necessary attitudes, the need for agent representation, the development of craft, and the importance of writers being one hundred percent committed to their careers. It lists their published books, which include Larsen's *Literary Agents: What They Do and How They Do It* and *How to Write a Book Proposal*. Pomada has a long-selling guide on places to take children in Northern California, and the pair collaborated on a series of beautifully illustrated books on Painted Ladies, restored Victorian houses painted in many colors. Naturally, being aimed at writers, the implication of the brochure is that they try Larsen/Pomada first.

Both were at New York houses in the sixties, Larsen at Morrow, Pyramid, Jove, and Bantam (during what he calls "the golden days, under Oscar Dystel and with a great group of people"), Pomada at Holt, with Eleanor Rawson, at David McKay, and then at Dial Press under Richard Baron. They met, they recall, at a Baker & Taylor New Book Preview at the old Statler-Hilton Hotel. They traveled together to the West Coast, found they liked San Francisco and decided to stay. It was 1970, and "There was absolutely nothing happening in California publishing at the time," says Larsen. Pomada went to an agency in search of jobs and didn't find one, though they discovered an interesting fact: the employment agency kept getting manuscripts from would-be writers who didn't know where to send them and thought anyone with the word "agent" in the title would do. "That gave us the idea that California needed us."

After Pomada started up as an agent in a couple of rooms in their apartment, where they still work, one of their first manuscripts turned out to be a hit. It was *A World Full of Strangers* by Cynthia Freeman, which Pomada sent to her old company, Holt. "When the editor-in-chief didn't want to publish it, three of the top executives who'd read it actually quit in anger," she says. When Arbor House and Bantam did eventually publish it, it became a best-seller. But things did not always run so smoothly for the neophytes. When Patty Hearst was kidnapped, Larsen went out after an instant book on the so-called Symbionese

Liberation Army that had done the deed. He sold it in four phone calls—but it took nineteen months to get it into print, and meanwhile other titles had exhausted the market.

"Fiction is 90 percent of what's written and 10 percent of what's sold; nonfiction is the other way around." (Larsen)

"Read and toss! Read and toss! And hope that someday there'll be something there." (Pomada)

But their proximity to so many aspiring authors (any agent will tell you that a good proportion of all unsolicited manuscripts come from California) proved beneficial in the long run. "New York has the reputation of being impenetrable, and many writers who had been intimidated by it found us," says Pomada. The people who eventually found them and signed on now number about two hundred, though people drop off, and others are always coming on board. "We send out about one hundred W-2 forms a year (showing some earnings)," says Larsen. "But there are a lot of one-book authors, and there are maybe forty active authors who write books on a regular basis. "They break down as about 75-25, or even 80-20, in favor of nonfiction. Pomada handles fiction, and nonfiction for women; Larsen does the rest. Pomada only accepted two novels from the many submissions by new authors last year, and Larsen adds the comment: "Fiction is 90 percent of what's written and 10 percent of what's sold. Nonfiction is the other way around."

Larsen has another startling motto: "For most nonfiction books with a wide national audience, the author's promotional plan can be eight times more important than the book's content in determining the editor, publisher, and deal." What he's saying is that, in an industry where new books have only a brief moment in the sun of attention their publication receives, those that don't have heavy promotional muscle behind them—much of it, of necessity, supplied by the author—are virtually doomed. In his *How to Write a Book Proposal,* there are three appendices reprinting proposals that succeeded in selling their respective books. Each of them is largely taken up with marketing and promotional plans in which the authors undertake extensive tours, speaking engagements, and offer to buy a considerable quantity of books from the publisher for resale—surely an irresistible offer.

Not every author will, or can, perform on this scale, but Larsen constantly stresses the need for an expansive and coherent marketing plan. "Back then, when we were in publishing," he says ruefully, "they complained we didn't think enough about marketing. Today's editors think of very little else. As usual, I guess, there was good news and bad news then. We could buy a book because we loved it; but most times we couldn't sell it." He adds: "The fundamental sea-change in publishing in recent years is that it has gone from being an editorially-driven business to a market-driven one."

It's scarcely a surprise, then, that many of the books they represent are books that seem to respond to the market, or are about aspects of marketing. Jay Conrad Levinson has done a series on what he calls Guerrilla Marketing for various publishers, and there are other books on money and marketing. Much of the nonfiction is of the self-help inspirational type, and the fiction is mainstream, or fantasy or science fiction series by the likes of Katharine Kerr and Lisa Mason.

More open than many agencies to new clients (they actually accept phone calls from them, a real rarity), Larsen and Pomada like their frequent trips to writers' conferences. "Nice to get out of the house," says Larsen, and Pomada adds: "It's great to be needed, and to remind yourself that writers are human beings too; we like to see the faces behind the books, and to meet other agents and editors."

But there's a certain amount of anxiety about the current state of the business, even from the normally upbeat Larsen. "Too many people think that because they have a computer they can write," he says of many would-be authors. "And of course there's always the difficulty of getting people on the phone. We demand a deadline for response to multiple submissions, usually five weeks, then they're out." He has a joke to elaborate on this theme. "Did you hear of the editor who told the agent he didn't do historical novels? 'It wasn't one when I sent it,' the agent said." Pomada chimes in sweetly: "But it's our job as agents to be patient, optimistic, and persistent."

Both agree that publishers often give writers shorter shrift than they once did. "If an author is on the A list, then goes to the B list, it's good-bye," says Larsen. "Still, publishing is our thing. No matter how awful it gets to be, other things are worse." On the future of publishing, he quotes from *The Leopard* by Giuseppe di Lampedusa: "If things are going to stay the same, then they're going to have to change." Pomada offers a vivid image for what they spend so much time doing, miming the actions: "Read and toss!" she declares. "Read and toss—and hope that someday there'll be something there."

"Sure," says Larsen. "The people in publishing have to be excited about books in the end, otherwise why are they there? Ever hear the definition of an optimist? An accordionist with a beeper."

WHO: Michael Larsen/Elizabeth Pomada

WHERE: 1029 Jones St.
San Francisco, CA 94109
415-673-0939

WHAT: General nonfiction (about 80 percent) and fiction (mostly women's).

LIST: Over one hundred active clients, including Cynthia Freeman, Jay Conrad Levinson, Katherine Kerr, Lisa Mason.

Member of AAR

Robert Lescher

Lescher & Lescher Ltd.

Bob Lescher, who works with his wife Susan as Lescher & Lescher Ltd. out of offices on Irving Place near New York's Union Square, is a thirty-year veteran agent who began his working life as an editor but then decided "I wanted to make my own mistakes."

Beginning in 1953, he spent nine years at what was then (and is now again) Henry Holt, then two years as executive editor at Houghton Mifflin, which he said "was very fusty then." The breaking point came when the well-known Broadway playwright S.N. Behrman wanted to do a book with Lescher and he discovered that none of his superiors at Houghton even knew who he was. "I figured if I was an agent I could say yes to a project that interested me, and refuse the ones that didn't. I wouldn't have to report to a committee. Everything at Houghton was done by committees then—and this was before the days of committees!"

Lescher is a broadly built, genial man with a relaxed, laid-back manner and a frequent smile that does not always seem to accord with what he is saying, hinting at some private internal joke. He dresses informally, in bulky sweaters and jeans, and looks some years younger than in his mid-sixties.

He didn't set up on his own as an agent right away after leaving Houghton, but called Carol Brandt at the Brandt & Brandt agency ("She'd told me the door was always open if ever I wanted to change sides"), and became an agent there in 1964. The arrangement was that if he left to go off on his own—which he did after a couple of years—he wouldn't take away with him any of the agency clients other than those he had brought aboard himself. Behrman was naturally one of the first to join him ("Authors, even well-known ones, didn't automatically have agents in those days") and they worked together for thirty-one years on a handshake. Mostly Lescher doesn't work on a contract basis with his clients, though some insist on one: Mamie Eisenhower did, for instance, and so did Benjamin Spock, who joined him in 1966 and whom Lescher represented until his death in 1998.

Nobel Prize–winning novelist and short story writer Isaac Bashevis Singer was another who felt he should have a contract, being a stickler for detail. "So I sent him one, a very informal one but full of good prose, which lasted for only a year, after which either of us could cancel. After a year Isaac called anxiously and said it was time to renew. I said we didn't really have to, and we went on that way until he died." He still represents Singer's estate.

When he began on his own, Lescher, like many fledgling agents making their way, shared office space: in his case, with agent Marie Rodell, whose phones and bookkeeper he also shared. Wife Susan came aboard very early on. She knew something about the work, having been in foreign rights at Doubleday, "and since she'd gone to secretarial school she could also type, which was something I badly needed."

Lescher can't imagine what it might be like starting out as an agent today. "We had a lot of luck people beginning now couldn't match. For one thing, I'd known a lot of people as an editor, so I could start out with some heavy hitters." Among them were artists seeking representation for books. David Levine the caricaturist was an early client, so was Andrew Wyeth, whose first book had been published by Houghton and who went on to become one of the big best-sellers among artists. "People, even well-known people, wanted someone to help clear up the mysteries of the publishing process." Hence a call out of the blue one day from Georgia O'Keeffe. "She asked if I represented the man who did the blades of grass, and if so she wanted to talk." She meant Wyeth, and they did talk, and Lescher represented her for one book before they agreed to part.

In the early days the agency did about 25 percent fiction (about the same proportion as most publishers), though there's probably less today. There was Singer, of course and Irish novelist Edna O'Brien until she succumbed, like many literary authors, to the lures of Andrew Wylie. It's sometimes hard, says Lescher, to figure how certain specialties develop. One of his specialties—books by noted financiers—may have started because as a young editor he handled Bernard Baruch's memoirs, which became a big best-seller in the 1950s. Much later came Boone Pickens and more recently the mysterious Central European billionaire George Soros (his lawyer called to set up representation).

A somewhat contradictory line was counter-establishment writers of books on the Vietnam war. Neil Sheehan, who came in through his wife (and fellow Pulitzer Prize–winner) Susan Sheehan, was one, Frances FitzGerald was another, and New York Times investigative reporter Seymour Hersh was a third. "I felt good about the books I handled in that subject area, and am still proud of them," Lescher says.

He feels an agent cannot get by on only one specialty, and Susan has developed what he calls "a tremendously valuable" one in upmarket cookbooks. It began, he says, with Marcella Hazan twenty years ago and now includes a number of successful food writers like Alice Waters of Berkeley's celebrated Chez Panisse, and journalists Patricia Welles and Molly O'Neill of the Times.

Altogether Lescher & Lescher is responsible for about fifty published books a year, from a stable that also includes the prolific Calvin Trillin, the *New Yorker's* Richard Harris, the United States rights of British biographer Michael Holroyd, and recent Random House star (and National Book Award–nominee) Jonathan Harr (*A Civil Action*).

How does he seek out new writers? He doesn't, very actively. "I don't go to writers' conferences any more to look, as I once did, as both an editor and a new agent. I'm not invited anymore, but back then it made a difference. I didn't always meet good writers among the students, but you came in contact with other members of the faculty doing good work." At one early such conference he recalls getting on a plane with science fiction author Madeleine L'Engle; they hit it off, and much later—in fact twenty years later—she left her agent to join Lescher.

He still receives a fair amount of over-the-transom mail from would-be authors, "mainly from aspiring novelists. They usually send a letter, a couple of pages describing the work. I'm not going to read a whole manuscript unless it's recommended to me by someone I know. I ask to see more from maybe three or four out of one hundred who write."

"I guess these author-agent relationships play themselves out, and maybe each gets the partner they ultimately deserve—rather like a marriage."

As an editor, he says, he would often try to put a promising author together with a subject he thought would make a good book, but "I find now that good writers mostly have their own subjects, they're not looking for something to write about." In terms of offering editorial assistance, "my job as an agent is to enhance the value of the product, so if you find something that needs improvement you'll say something. But the vast majority of my writers don't need any editorial help."

Like publishing, he finds agenting now more aggressively competitive than it used to be. He has lost one or two clients to poaching by other agents, but is philosophical about it. "I guess these author-agent relationships play themselves out, and maybe each gets the partner they ultimately deserve—rather like a marriage." The chief problem he encounters is one of editorial responsiveness. "As recently as a couple of years ago an editor working on a project with you would suggest lunch; they don't do that any more." Often he has to make more follow-up calls, write more letters, than he would like, in order to evoke a response. "Are editors really too busy, are they getting so much publishable material they feel they don't have to bother? Maybe this new casual behavior towards agents is something that's coming down from the top, but it bothers me, the feeling that things are being decided over our heads."

WHO: Lescher & Lescher Ltd.
Robert Lescher, Susan Lescher

WHERE: 67 Irving Pl.
New York, NY 10003
212-529-1790; fax: 212-529-2716

WHAT: General nonfiction (about 75 percent, including a strong cookbook specialty) and fiction.

LIST: About 120 clients producing as many as fifty books a year, including Neil Sheehan, Frances FitzGerald, Seymour Hersh, Marcella Hazan, Calvin Trillin, Richard Harris, Patricia Welles, Jonathan Harr, Madeleine L'Engle, George Soros, Boone Pickens, the estates of Benjamin Spock, Isaac Bashevis Singer.

Member of AAR

Ellen Levine
Ellen Levine Literary Agency, Inc.

Levine, who achieved a special kind of fame not usually given to agents when she was involved in the fantastically successful sales of Nicholas Evans's *The Horse Whisperer* to Delacorte/Dell and Hollywood (although, as she points out, she was not its primary agent), is a slim, intense woman with dark hair, a pale face and piercing eyes, which gaze from behind fashionably styled glasses. She is in many ways the very image of the successful New York career woman, focused and sharp.

After graduation from Brooklyn College ("in the days when it was still a top school," she hastens to add) she wanted, as people so often do, to "do something in books," and an agency sent her as an assistant to David Segal, an editor at New American Library, which at that time had an ambitious program of quality fiction. He gave her books to edit that included *A Fan's Notes,* the celebrated novel by Frederick Exley, and work by William Gass, Cynthia Ozick, and Alice Adams. That was enough to solidify her ambition to be an editor, and she moved on to Harper & Row, hoping for such a promotion. "But it was harder for a woman then, and I couldn't get anywhere."

She heard of a job at the Paul Reynolds agency, the oldest in the United States, which wanted someone to sell magazine rights. Levine, however, wanted to find her own writers. "I remember writing to the people who edited a newsletter written and edited by a group of prisoners at Illinois State Penitentiary." She asked them if they wanted to collaborate on a book, and the result was *An Eye for an Eye,* published by Holt. "I got about ten writers that way, by casting around, and even began to sell a few books, but the agency didn't want me to spend my time that way, so I was stymied again."

Perry Knowlton, the head of Curtis Brown, called in 1971, asking if she wanted to join that agency, and she gladly accepted. The first writers she dealt with there were Garrison Keillor and Russell Banks, neither as well known then as they later became. "Banks said that when he came to see me he was expecting to see this tough New York agent, and it turned out to be just a kid in a miniskirt with a tiny office." But at last she had the opportunity to create her own list, and she stayed at the agency for nine years, learning the ropes and building a list of more than thirty clients.

She started her own agency in 1980, with just a part-time secretary, in premises rented to her by an accountant friend, placing her office between those of two of his staff accountants, who were constantly feuding: "I was sort of a buffer between them." Although she took a number of clients with her, "it was tough at first, because Curtis Brown was where their earlier deals were, and in effect I was starting from scratch." Perhaps as a result of that experience, she remains interested in finding new clients, and helping develop younger writers, though most come to her now by recommendation.

She used to go to writers' conferences to scope out new talent, particularly in her earlier days, though no longer has the time—or the need. She does remember one, in Oklahoma, where she encountered a writer who wanted to do an inspirational book about how she found God through her work. What was her work? Levine asked. "She was a hairdresser, and she wanted to call her book *The Power Behind the Comb.*" Then there was an old man who had written a complete history of the United States in verse... She takes a mischievous delight in such aberrations.

Levine now has offices just off Park Avenue South, a staff of eight, plus two part-timers and a bookkeeper. Her key staffers include Elizabeth Kaplan, who works with her as a full agent, Diana Finch for serial rights, Louis Quayle for foreign and audio rights. The balance of her clients is about 50-50 between fiction and nonfiction, with Levine herself concentrating more on the fiction. It is a starry list, including, in fiction Banks and Keillor (both of whom she retained), National Book Award–nominee Larry Heinemann, Mary Morris, Christina Garcia, Carolyn Heilbrun (who also writes thrillers as Amanda Cross), Rosa Guy, Joan Chase Martinez, Michael Ondaatje (author of *The English Patient,* whom she has represented for fifteen years), Marilyn Robinson, Jane Urquhart, and publicity director turned novelist Jane Heller. In nonfiction there's Todd Gitlin, Michael Gross, Jamake Highwater, Jonathan Kwitny, Colette Dowling, and Christopher Anderson.

"It seems to me that publishers want everything served up on a silver platter. There aren't so many editors around with superior editing skills, and in general I sense a shrinking market. Too many people are trying to do too many things, and there's a sense of no one in charge."

Her chief problem with publishers is that "they're so unsure about their decisions, they can get so easily led by the marketing department. An author may have won awards, got excellent reviews consistently, but poor sales on one title can doom his next. It seems to me they want everything served up on a silver platter. There aren't so many editors around with superior editing skills, and in general I sense a shrinking market. Too many people are trying to do too many things, and there's a sense of no one in charge."

As with so many effective agents, she conveys a sense of impatience at the perceived inefficiency with which they have to constantly deal.

WHO: Ellen Levine Literary Agency, Inc.
Ellen Levine, Elizabeth Kaplan

WHERE: 15 East 26th St. (Ste. 1801)
New York, NY 10010
212-889-0620; fax: 212-725-4501

WHAT: General fiction and nonfiction, about 50-50, strong in politics on the nonfiction side.

LIST: About one hundred active clients, including Garrison Keillor, Russell Banks, Larry Heinemann, Mary Morris, Carolyn Heilbrun, Marilyn Robinson, Michael Ondaatje, Jane Urquhart, Jane Heller, Jamake Highwater, Jonathan Kwitny, Todd Gitlin, Colette Dowling, Christopher Anderson.

Member of AAR

Gloria Loomis
Watkins Loomis Agency, Inc.

Although the agency is actually known as Watkins Loomis, it is, and has been for years, very much Gloria Loomis's own agency; she kept the Watkins name, she says, because "I loved the idea of the continuity, the author history there. There were typescripts in the office of Virginia Woolf, with her own handwritten corrections!"

It all began with Ann Watkins, whom Loomis described as "a hard-drinking matriarch," and who founded the Watkins agency in 1908—one of the first in the country—and passed it along to her son Armitage. It was Armitage for whom Loomis first went to work as an assistant in 1971. "It represented the great British agencies and had an amazing list, including Dorothy L. Sayers, Josephine Tey, early Roald Dahl (and his estate), Kay Boyle, the Edith Wharton estate, Beryl Markham, lots of Peter De Vries. There were lots of properties, but no young writers."

Loomis, a petite, dark-eyed woman who speaks in enthusiastic bursts, married (and later divorced) Bob Loomis, a senior editor at Random House, and for a while her career was put on hold. Then "I moved to Europe, built a house in Spain, and then I came back and got serious."

On her return she became a partner with Armitage Watkins and Peggy Caulfield, in the agency's old offices on Park Avenue. Later, she moved to East 35th Street, where the agency is today (for some years the office shared a building with William F. Buckley's *National Review*). Then Watkins retired, and in 1980 Loomis became president.

As she began to build her own list, she went for the younger authors she had missed at the old agency: Stanley Kaufman and Jerzy Kosinski were friends who sent some of their promising students as early clients, and she also began to take on younger protégés of authors the agency already represented, including students of Maureen Howard and Frederick Tuten (Walter Mosley, now one of her star authors, was one). She had an interest in against-the-grain journalists, and Raymond Bonner, of the *New York Times*, brought in Bill McKibben. The nun Helen Prejean (*Dead Man Walking*) was another. So was R.W.B. Lewis, and Betty Fussell, who sent husband and wife Nicholas Fox Weber and Katharine Weber. Performance artist Anna Deavere Smith is a friend of Mosley's, Roger Rosenblatt of Kaufman's, Cornel West came in through Michael Lerner. There is a strong African-American and minority accent to the list, which also includes Kiran Desai, Edwidge Danticat (one of Oprah's newer book club choices), and Junot Diaz, all brought in by her "wonderful" associate Nicole Aragi. And so it goes.

Things didn't always work out. Arianna Huffington (then Stassounopoulos) came in after her book on Picasso, through Francois Gilot, and they were together for one book *Fourth Basic Instinct*, but "Arianna came up with notions I didn't like," and they agreed to part company. But art and architecture has always been an interest, and her coup in getting the *Journals* of iconic Mexican artist Frida Kahlo a few years back shows how the grapevine works. Colin Eisler, the husband of client Benita Eisler (who is currently writing a biography of Lord Byron), knew people at the Kahlo/Rivera Trust in Mexico who had rights to the diaries, and sent them the way of his wife's agent;

Loomis sold the journals to Abrams in a big deal for an art-related book. "You never know where things are going to come from," says Loomis, waving an arm around at the book-lined walls. "Each book in this room has some sort of connection, came to me through someone I know."

She seems to want to give an impression of inspired amateurism. "I see the agenting business partly as a kind of graduate school education. If something interests me and I really believe in it, I'll go for it. It's tap dancing in the dark, but it's worked well so far."

Loomis's list is about 60 percent nonfiction to 40 percent fiction, though it fluctuates from time to time. "I'm very careful about what I take on," she declares, then goes on to enthuse about a couple of first novels, and a well-received novel, *Skull Session* by Daniel Hecht, which Aragi retrieved from the slush pile.

"I don't want publishers to lose their shirts on my clients. But I've found that if they really love a book enough they'll take it—though not for the famous six-figure advances! I have so many negative thoughts about those six-figure prices for goofy things, and all the good books they supplant."

She is not proactive in the sense of putting authors together with subjects she thinks deserve a book. "Most of them come up with ideas of their own, though sometimes they're ideas that just don't work." Working with journalists as much as she does, she finds their first book is often hard—"they're not used to being able to expand."

Agents, she thinks, are working harder than ever these days, not just to sell their clients' books, but to set those clients straight about the facts of publishing life. "I think today they listen more when we tell them something is not quite ready yet. You often have to go through several drafts before you get something just right. And I find I often have to lecture my clients on the realities of the situation—that the placement of their books in the store, for instance, often involves a payment from the publisher."

She has ongoing difficulties with publishers. "I've always been a scrapper, but I've learned to pick my shots very carefully. Contracts have to be done with extra care these days—you can't take anything for granted as you used to. Royalty statements are always a problem, sometimes without any relation to reality, though some publishers have reluctantly begun to do some of the things I've asked." Another difficulty she finds lately is a "timidity in reprinting—they're worried about any new printing that might put the book in the red, even if it seems called for. I'm not insensitive—I don't want publishers to lose their shirts on my clients. But I've found that if they really love a book enough, they'll take it—though not for those famous six-figure advances! I have so many negative thoughts about those six-figure prices for goofy things, and all the good books they supplant."

Her own tastes run to literary biography, good journalism, fiction with a distinctive flavor, and she's happy to see signs of a resurgence in such things at some houses and with some editors. She sees herself as "intensely pragmatic," will painstakingly take an author through every phase of the process up to publication; and "I'd rather someone go to the right house than drain the last nickel." She only does auctions very occasionally, and tends to send out manuscripts or proposals in small rather than large batches, and sometimes to only one editor she has decided is ideal. "But of course these days no one can buy a book all by themselves."

Despite the nature of her almost determinedly anti-commercial (by conventional standards) list, Loomis remains an optimist—"infused, like a fool, with hope about writers and writing. You have to love it; that's all that can keep you going."

WHO: Watkins Loomis Agency, Inc.
Gloria Loomis, Nicole Aragi

WHERE: 133 East 35th St. (Ste. 1)
New York, NY 10016
212-532-0080; fax: 212-889-0506
email: watkloomis@aol.com

WHAT: General fiction and nonfiction, 60 percent fiction, including literary and Third World authors; art, journalism significant on nonfiction side.

LIST: About sixty active writers, including Maureen Howard, Frederick Tuten, Walter Mosley, Raymond Bonner, Helen Prejean, Bill McKibben, R.W.B Lewis, Katharine Weber, Anna Deavere Smith, Roger Rosenblatt, Cornel West, Edwidge Danticat, Junot Diaz, Kiran Desai, Benita Eisler.

Barbara Lowenstein

Lowenstein Associates Inc

Lowenstein is representative of the tough, no-nonsense school of (largely) nonfiction agents who have adapted well to the vagaries of today's marketplace, though she still remembers the easier past times with some nostalgia. Well-tailored in a white suit, she moves decisively around her suite of offices near the Flatiron building, and lays out her activities firmly.

Lowenstein got her first job toward the end of the 1960s working as a secretary-assistant at the Sterling Lord Agency. They had a thoroughly hip list at the time: Jack Kerouac, Martin Duberman, Terry Southern, Ken Kesey—"God, I couldn't wait to get up in the morning, it was so exciting!" After a few years, however, as the sixties faded, so did the thrill, so Lowenstein took a year off to travel around the world, and returned into a publishing spot. She worked for marketer supreme Walter Zacharius at Lancer Books, where she headed the trade paperback Larchmont line. "We did all sorts of self-help books—crafts, cookbooks, psychology, women's books, diet books. The books were mostly illustrated, and I'd get the authors and illustrators together, and I'd go to crafts fairs and all kinds of expos to see what was needed. I loved it."

Late in the 1970s she formed her own agency, taking some authors from Lancer, but finding most of her own, putting together series fiction packages, selling some rights. "Soon I was making more than when I'd been employed. But it was so easy then. There were fourteen paperback houses, God knows how many hardcover publishers, and when they started a new men's series or whatever, they would call and ask you for ten titles, and I'd round up three authors and we'd go to work to provide them. I was involved with the launching of the first adult Western series. We'd sell at least one hundred books a year. Everything was volume, and you were happy if they paid $10,000 per title; you could make a big profit on that, with enough of them. It was nothing like now, when you have to depend on big deals. But that all lasted less than ten years."

"Nonfiction authors now need good credentials, like television shows, seminars. Yes, I know it used to be the other way around: first you made your name with the book, then the rest came along. But not any more."

In the early eighties she began to collect some star authors, some of whom stayed for many years, some of whom are still around. They included Ishmael Reed, whom she found at a writer's conference, Tim Cahill, Jack Kramer, the dean of gardening book writers, David Rorvik (whose *In His Image: The Cloning of a Man* caused a big stir at the time, though it would seem tame now), celebrity biographer Charles Higham, Warren Hinckle. She also began to make alliances with medical institutions that created major trade reference books: the American Cancer Society, the Academy of Pediatrics, the Columbia Medical Guide, the Mount Sinai Nutrition Book, and the like.

She hired two agents: one, Nancy Yost, does highly commercial fiction—women's fiction, mysteries, and thrillers—and has writers who have been nominated for many prestigious awards. One of her finds, two sisters who write legal thrillers as Perri O'Shaughnessy, have hit the *New York Times* best-seller list. The other agent, Eileen Cope, concentrates on African-American and spirituality topics, and has brought in such titles as *Watch Me Fly* by Myrlie Evers-Williams (Medgar Evers's widow).

Among Lowenstein's current authors are Barbara Keesling, who does sex books, Walter Pierpaoli (*The Melatonin Miracle*), the sexy-novel writer Laura Reese (*Topping from Below* and *Panic Snap*), Pulitzer Prize–winning journalist Michael Waldholz, and Lawrence Naumoff (*A Plan for Women*). She estimates a ratio of 25 percent fiction to 75 percent nonfiction, and says she's "always looking for people. I'd never give up reading new stuff. That would be death." As a veteran packager, Lowenstein looks for experts to provide their knowledge, and writers who can lick the material into shape: "I'm trying to move some authors away from the idea of having their name on the book."

She insists that publishers are now only looking for celebrity and/or expert-driven books with obvious and built-in marketing appeal. "They need good credentials, like television shows, seminars. Yes, I know, it used to be the other way around: first you made your name with the book, then the rest came along, but not any more." The books she takes on "have to be very market-driven and very carefully targeted, and, yes, that means you take on fewer books than you'd like to."

Lowenstein is not one to complain about publisher practices, giving the impression that she simply doesn't allow them to get away with anything. "I don't have a problem with slow payment, and if an author is having financial problems waiting for the advance, we'll help them out." Likewise with editorial response times. "We sell our books very quickly, usually within a few days. We send out extremely good proposals—we work on them until they're as good as we can make them—and editors will usually look at ours first. But I'll always call first, to try to get them excited. If necessary I'll take around a tape of the author to show television potential, or even the author himself." Also, unlike most agents, she plans to expand soon beyond her present staff of six. "I'm hiring two new agents. I want this agency to grow; there's a whole new generation coming up of young writers, editors, and readers, and I want to be ready for them."

WHO: Lowenstein Associates Inc
Barbara Lowenstein, Nancy Yost, Eileen Cope

WHERE: 121 West 27th St. (Ste. 601)
New York, NY 10001
212-206-1630; fax: 212-727-0280

WHAT: General nonfiction (about 75 percent) and fiction.

LIST: About one hundred active clients, including Charles Higham, Jack Kramer, Perri O'Shaughnessy, Myrlie Evers-Williams, Barbara Keesling, Laura Reese, Michael Waldholz, Lawrence Naumoff.

Member of AAR

Carol Mann

Carol Mann Agency

"I didn't know what an agent was when I started out," says Carol Mann in her airy, bright office with big windows on lower Fifth Avenue. "Or if I did have a hint of an idea, I thought of them as glamorous people who wielded enormous power." She is a slight, dark-haired woman who seems somewhat remote behind fashionable wire-frame glasses. Tentative and rather cautious at first, she warms up as the interview proceeds.

Educated at Smith College and then Columbia, Mann taught private school for a while after graduation, then went into educational promotion at Avon. "It sounds like an odd thing, but Avon at that time was hardly typical," she says. She was promoting the house's titles into the school market, then was persuaded to become a children's editor. When a new publisher came aboard in 1976 she was fired, which she now thinks of as "the best thing that ever happened to me," though she didn't think so then. For a while she drifted, doing some speech writing, and reading for mass market publishers, before becoming the agent for the first international-prize-winning Israeli children's book author: "For a time I had two cards, one as an agent, one as an editor."

When she did begin agenting seriously, in 1978, it was mostly with children's authors. "I guess I did it because that's what I knew, and there were few agents in the field. I hadn't wanted to be a children's editor, so I was an agent."

As she began to develop an adult list she did it by encouraging journalist friends to do books. Examples of such are a tennis reporter with a book on the pro circuit, and a black beauty book. Her first big contract was for astrophysicist Robert Jastrow, a book explaining the mysteries of the universe. From the start she was a proactive agent, putting authors together with subjects she thought they could handle well. "I developed a reputation for finding academics who could cross over into trade books, people with expertise in a field who could make it generally accessible."

But it was still on a very small scale; she worked out of her studio apartment. "I had to get a convertible couch so I could get the bed out of the way, because I was getting crowded out by manuscripts." She was "not exactly methodical" in her search for new clients. She went to a couple of writers' conferences, ended up picking up a fitness book indirectly at one, but found she got more from meeting the editors attending than from the authors themselves. It took about ten years before she felt there was a reliable cash flow, before, says Mann, "I felt I'd arrived, that people knew my name."

Since then her annual take has either improved or stayed the same—and, in fact, the past year had been particularly notable. Client James Tobin, a Detroit newspaperman, had won the National Book Critics Circle award for his book *Ernie Pyle's War,* which had helped her to sell his next book, on the Wright Brothers and their first flight, for a greatly increased advance. "That's one of the great pleasures of a job like this, to be able to call someone like Jim and tell him he could quit his job at the paper and write full-time. It's great to be able to make it easier for someone to be a writer." Most of her list is still nonfiction, but a notable acquisition was Paul Auster, who while seeking an agent met a friend of hers in Paris in the early 1980s and got recommended. Busy with movies as well as books, he is one of those occasional American writers who do better in Europe (where he is a considerable cult figure whose every new work is eagerly awaited) than at home. Other notable clients include *New York Times* correspondent Fox Butterfield (*All God's Children*), divorce expert Dr. Judith Wallerstein, with two best-selling books on marriage and divorce, and best-selling essayist Shelby Steele.

Another recent success has been the signing of a highly lucrative four-book deal for Lorraine Johnson-Coleman, a National Public Radio star, which she uses as an example of the range of deals her agency makes. "I can be wrestling with a university press for an extra $500, or hashing out the fine points on a seven-figure deal with a big trade house. I can be as excited at placing a first novel (like client Mark Jacobs's recent well-received *Stone Cowboy*) with Soho Press as in Tobin winning the NBCC."

Her view of the agent's role: "It's our job to put the author in good hands, then hope and pray that the editor doesn't leave; after that to push and guide, to hope words in the right place will help with publicity and promotion." There's also a great deal to do getting a project ready for sale, and Mann does a lot of editing and polishing on proposals. Unsolicited material still pours in, and every now and again she finds something. "Recently I got a letter so well written that I couldn't resist asking for a proposal, though it was about country and western music, something I know nothing about. Then I sold it to an editor who said he only did 'big' books, but who was also drawn by the sheer quality of the writing."

She finds today's environment much more competitive, and tries to create in her office a non-stressful environment by bringing in "congenial colleagues"—in her case former editors who had left the competitive in-house fray for flexible family time. This heightened in-house tension, she feels, makes it harder for editors to do the kind of job they used to do in bringing along new talent. "Everyone needs a 'platform' today, like Johnson-Coleman's audience at NPR, a built-in readership; perhaps it's the pressure from the chains, who knows?" In any case, she finds there are books she could have sold ten years ago that can no longer command any advance. "I used to think that any good book would get published, but these days the mid-list is really problematic. But perhaps the resurgence of small press publishing and the fact that university presses are broadening their coverage, means that mid-list nonfiction is not in as much danger as fiction."

"There were too many books being published that shouldn't have been, and with the correction it's looking healthier in some ways. But the downside is that those corrections were made by the numbers-crunchers, not the editorial staff. There's a real danger now that a passionate editor may no longer be able to publish books for which an economic argument can't be made."

Getting contracts and payment in reasonable time, she finds, depends on how much pressure she creates, as well as on the publisher. "Sometimes it's a problem with the editor simply not pushing, sometimes it's a case of everyone under pressure, and not enough hands to do the work." There are many ways a book, once accepted, can fall between the cracks. "A book can die because of poor presentation to sales, or an editor not knowing which buttons to press. And there are books that senior people don't have time for, or the inclination for, and the younger editors who take them on don't have the clout to make them work. I have one like that right now. There's a saving grace when senior people are looking over the shoulders of the younger ones, but you can't always depend on that.

"You learn by doing, and junior people used to have to learn everything it took to be a publisher, but there are lots of things they simply don't know anymore, like sending out promo copy and cover art to be approved before they're finalized. It's a question of publishing manners, and in some places this is taught, in others not. At some places you don't need to put the need for this kind of consultation in the contract, at others it's essential."

Mann feels corrections in the publishing world that were overdue have now been made. "There were too many books published that shouldn't have been, and with the correction it's looking healthier in some ways. But the downside is that those corrections were made by the numbers-crunchers, not the editorial staff. There's a real danger now that a passionate editor may no longer be able to publish books for which an economic argument can't be made."

WHO: Carol Mann Agency

WHERE: 55 Fifth Ave.
New York, NY 10003
212-206-5635; fax: 212-675-4809
email: cmlass@aol.com

WHAT: General nonfiction and fiction, about 80 percent nonfiction.

LIST: About thirty-five clients, including James Tobin, Dr. Judith Wallerstein, Robert Jastrow, Fox Butterfield, Waris Dirie, Lorraine Johnson-Coleman, Paul Auster, Marita Golden, Mark Jacobs.

Member of AAR

Janet and Jillian Manus

Manus & Associates Literary Agency Inc.

Mother and daughter work together as Manus & Associates—but three thousand miles apart, with mother Janet on East 57th Street (a fashionable street for agents) in New York, daughter Jillian out of an office in Palo Alto, California. They are a handsome couple, the mother a well-groomed lady in her middle years, the daughter a tall, statuesque blonde who looks closer to Hollywood than Palo Alto. "Here she comes, Miss America," said Janet fondly as Jillian arrived to take part in the joint interview at a Chinese restaurant popular with celebrities on the ground floor of the CBS building in Manhattan.

Jillian had just come from seeing Warner Books chief Larry Kirshbaum, saying she had asked for $400,000 to take a book she was representing "off the table" (meaning a pre-emptive bid, after which she would not accept other offers). She was still waiting to see whether he would agree, as he was very interested, but meanwhile was going ahead showing the book to someone else that afternoon. It seemed an odd sort of book to be commanding such potential big money: it was a self-published self-help book she had found at a writers' conference in San Diego, and the author had sold four thousand copies locally in just a few weeks; now she was planning to take him national. It's a technique she has applied on several occasions with success.

Mother and daughter are both frequent speakers at such conferences, and in fact Jillian is arranging the agents who will be present at the prestigious (and much sought after, by publishing people and writers alike) Maui Writers Conference held every Labor Day weekend at a luxury resort on the Hawaiian island. They have rather different motivations, however. Whereas Janet says that there are areas she wants to develop, "and I go after certain types of authors, mostly journalists, and the occasional gem in fiction," and doesn't have time to read much "slush," Jillian declares, in her breathy, bright-eyed manner: "I love discovering new talent. New writers are easier to work with, I get inspiration from them, their freshness of vision; and I love introducing new clients to publishers." As a result of what she calls her "enlightened upbringing," she has "great respect for writers, who sacrifice such a lot for what they do."

Both are strongly oriented toward books of special interest to women. Jillian's first success as an agent was selling Dr. Richard Marrs's *Fertility Book* for $250,000. As a self-described "pro-choice Republican," she says, "I want to see books that empower women, in health, parenting, overcoming adversity." On the fiction side her appetite is for big thrillers with strong movie or television possibilities (her client list marks the fiction entries that have been sold for the screen—though not necessarily made, options being what they are—and they are many) or commercial women's fiction. Janet likes what she calls "issue-based" books, especially ones dealing with injustice, though she hastens to add: "I'm not running the agency just as a good cause; they have to be publishable."

Janet began the agency about sixteen years ago, partly by accident. Her husband is an entertainment lawyer who also acted as a counsel for Bantam Books as well as the Guinness Book of Records, so book deals were always part of the atmosphere surrounding her. Then, after she had made a trip to

England, an author called and said he wanted someone to represent him in the United States. As a result, since she already did some reading for various publishers, she agreed to try it, and gradually began to build up a sideline in representing rights for British and Australian publishers here. At first it was mostly movie and television business, but eventually she began to get some authors too. It took about five years, she says, to build it to the point where it was a profitable living.

"Publishing is now very formulaic, and meanwhile smaller publishers are gaining strength with mid-list books. I find I'm taking on more independently produced books and making deals for them with big publishers." (Jillian)

Enter Jillian. "I grew up at the dinner table always hearing my folks talking deals and books, but no one urged me to go into the business." She had been, she says, a competitive gymnast as a girl, loved sports—"I learned all about strategy, teamwork, and the thrill of winning." She also began writing in college, and after graduation went into a series of jobs, first as an intern at ICM in the television department, then when she was offered a production spot at Warner Brothers, she moved out to the West Coast. Spots at Universal and De Laurentis followed and gradually, as she found herself looking at a lot of books for potential movie development, she began to learn about the book business. She sees, in fact, a lot of parallels between the way the two industries have developed: "The book business now is like the movie business in the eighties, when it was looking for concept, formula; now there's more of a balance between the big studios and the independents. Publishing is now very formulaic, and meanwhile smaller publishers are gaining strength with mid-list books. I find I'm taking on more independently produced books and making deals for them with big publishers."

After a few years in the movie business, a spell working for a Swiss company that backed media ventures, and as associate publisher of two start-up national magazines, "my mother asked me what I really wanted to do, and I said: 'Work with writers.' " She was living on the West Coast at the time, but her mother said "You can be an agent anywhere," so she opened up near her home in Palo Alto. She made a formal debut in the book business with Janet on a trip to the American Booksellers Association convention in Miami in 1992. "It's a family agency," she says. "There's no answering to a corporation. We have loyalty to each other, as partners, and perhaps our authors figure we'll give loyalty to them."

According to Janet, "I brought in Jillian originally thinking I would turn the agency over to her eventually, and I still expect to do so." Jillian: "Mother will never stop working."

They have contrasting styles. Janet describes herself as "a good ideas, concepts person," whereas Jillian likes to line-edit, and does a considerable amount of it on half of what she sends out. "I always have a marketing plan to help publicize the book," she adds. Janet finds she has to work three times as hard now as ten years ago to make a decent deal for a book, and Jillian agrees that these days "we have to do much of the publisher's marketing for them." Both work very hard at cover letters, for both fiction and nonfiction, taking each through several drafts, spending up to two days on a letter to get it right. Jillian declares: "A cover letter should do for fiction what a proposal does for nonfiction." She will create two-minute videotapes for any author with a six-figure deal, and offers this interviewer with approval an outline by *Chicken Soup* co-author Jack Canfield of how he spends 90 percent of his waking moments promoting his series of books into the worldwide success they have become.

In addition to Janet, Jillian feels fortunate in having had two powerful mentors in the publishing business, in Simon & Schuster's Michael Korda and Random's Peter Gethers. "They always were able to give me a sense of the publisher's point of view, what publishers are *really* looking for, as compared to what they say they're looking for." What both Manuses seem to feel they are looking for are inspirational stories; as Jillian puts it, of her movie days seeking properties: "They always wanted me to buy things that end in hope. I still follow that." So books like Janice Burns's *Sarah's Song,* sold to Warner for a quarter million, is said to have helped a woman in a hospital with AIDS, and Janet's Edgar-winning true-crime author Carlton Stowers's *Sins of the Son* had proved therapeutic for its subject, the father of a boy convicted of murder.

The list, not large but very well-paying, is about 50-50 fiction and nonfiction. Janet does occasional gardening books and cookbooks, though neither are specialty areas. She will also do the occasional mystery, whereas both go for thrillers. Neither are interested in category fiction—romance, science fiction, horror—but both express a wish to open up more to multicultural books and gay and lesbian subjects.

As befits an agency with what seems like considerable clout in today's high-concept publishing marketplace, the Manuses like to use their bargaining power for the author's benefit. "If a publisher puts a promotional budget in a contract we'll take less, and we've left money on the table (i.e., taken less) to find the house we want, one that will do best for our author," Jillian declares.

WHO: Manus & Associates Literary Agency Inc.
Janet Manus, Jillian Manus

WHERE: Janet: 417 East 57th St. (Ste. 5D)
New York, NY 10022
212-644-8020; fax: 212-644-3374
Jillian: 430 Cowper St.
Palo Alto, CA 94301
415-617-4556

WHAT: General fiction and nonfiction, divided about 50–50, upbeat, commercial; often take independently produced books to bigger publishers.

LIST: About forty active clients, including Dr. Richard Marrs, Janice Burns, Carlton Stowers.

Member of AAR

Denise Marcil
Denise Marcil Literary Agency Inc.

Well-groomed and utterly self-possessed, Denise Marcil is a prime example of agent as skilled and savvy businessperson, one who has learned to change with the market and adapt swiftly to its changing needs. She is also one of the very few encountered in interviewing for this book who seems to have a coherent business plan, which she regularly reviews, complete with targets.

Perhaps rather surprisingly under those circumstances, she is also one of the most receptive to new clients, and estimates she gets as many as a third of them from submissions. "I get piles of query letters, and if I'm interested I just ask to look at a partial manuscript," she says. "I can always tell from the first ten pages if something's going to work or not." She also goes to writers' conferences, on a selective basis. "You never know where the next big writer is coming from—and the best part of the job is still selling that first book." As an example, she describes how she recently got a letter from an American living in England with a copy of a book, *Your Best Year Yet,* that had been published there and sold quite well. "Because the author was establishing a platform in the United States with workshops and infomercials, I was able to make a nice six-figure sale here," she says.

Marcil was an English major at Skidmore, and her first job was as an editorial assistant at Avon in Peter Mayer's day: "It was a great place to work." But after only eighteen months she had an offer to move to Simon & Schuster to do women's fiction, at twice the salary. After a time, however, her mentor there left and so did Marcil, to a job with agent Bobbe Siegel, and "much to my surprise I found I loved selling. Since I had editorial skills too, I thought I'd try it on my own, and foolishly quit."

That first year, 1977, she sold only one book, and was only able to keep going because she also had a part-time job with a McGraw-Hill trade magazine. She went to all the writers' workshops and classes she could, wrote some articles herself, represented some authors for magazine pieces. "It wasn't financially smart, but it made me good contacts with editors, and finally they sent me some great journalists." What finally turned her agency around was the discovery, through an article, of American Women's Economic Development Corporation, which ran courses teaching women how to enter business. Marcil took the course, learned how to do business and marketing plans, and has faithfully done them and reviewed them every year since.

"As the market changed, I did too. You have to adjust to the marketplace."

As part of her business plan, she examined what she had been selling, found she had sold thirteen romances in the past year, and vowed to double it. "Next year I sold thirty-three, and quickly became one of the top agents for romances." She is swift to reject the suggestion that these could not have been very profitable: "They were all lucrative in terms of royalties, and some of the writers have broken out since into mainstream best-sellers." And the volume is phenomenal: Marcil estimates that in twenty years agenting she has sold something like fifteen hundred titles.

She learned to specialize—"As the market changed, I did
too." She gave up on mainstream fiction as "impossible to sell,
no matter how good it is," and began to do practical nonfiction
books, "books that helped change people's lives," parenting
books, consumer guides, which she describes as "backlist cash
cows." After reading and admiring Tom Peters's *In Search of
Excellence* she began to do business books; and with her usual
thoroughness she wrote to universities like Stanford and
University of South Carolina asking business professors if they
had books they wanted to do. They did, and titles like *Getting
Rich in America* and *The Connective Edge* followed. "By the fifth
year I found I was really making money." Until a couple of years
ago her sixty-odd clients represented 70–80 percent fiction,
mostly women's, with a scattering of mysteries. In the past two
years nonfiction has risen to about 40 percent. Ever economical,
Marcil still works out of her West End Avenue apartment. She's
looked from time to time at office space, "but I don't want to
spend the money. If an author wants an agent with a big office,
I'm the wrong person."

As an entrepreneur, Marcil repeats, "you have to adjust to
the marketplace," and recounts some of the dizzying swoops that
followed. Paperback houses consolidated, cut their lists dramatically. From the late eighties into the early nineties, there was a
boom in business books, then editors started to complain that
the chain buyers found they weren't moving at the stores, so
they stopped doing them. "Suddenly they've started coming
back again." The eighties' boom in romance dipped toward the
end of the decade, then it came back for a while, it's now down
again. Spirituality titles began as a New Age offshoot, then
moved in a religious direction.

Because so much of her living depends on paperback fiction, Marcil took the unusual step of inviting a group of spe-
cialist publishers out to breakfast last year to ask them what was
happening. Their diagnosis: the market now depends on a handful of wholesale distributors who are primarily interested in

incentive offers, and they find the shelf space allotted to such titles is much reduced.

"Lots of people complain it's not fun any more, that the spontaneity is gone," says Marcil. "It's the power of the chains, making gambles much more expensive, so you have to think things out and plan them more carefully, doing a great cover for a book to make more of it, for instance." As for editors, "they're far more cautious now about losing their jobs, so they won't make risky calls. You find that less and less are they ready to go out and fight for a book. And it's amazing how little editing is done—even if they want to do it, the boss tells them not to waste time on it, he's only interested in acquisition. I heard of one who was told to double the number of books he acquired, and not to bother with anything else," they would hire a developmental editor to do the actual editing. "As a result, agents themselves have to do more and more editing, or have their authors hire freelance editors to do it for them."

It doesn't seem like an intelligent use of staff, and it's plain the highly pragmatic Marcil would like to see things organized differently; still, her strength is to make the best of things as they are, and she has been highly successful with that approach.

WHO: Denise Marcil Literary Agency Inc.

WHERE: 685 West End Ave. (Ste. 9C)
New York, NY 10025
212-932-3110

WHAT: Commercial fiction about 60 percent (a lot of romance), and mostly self-help nonfiction; particularly open to new writers in these fields.

LIST: About sixty active writers, including Anita Bunkley, Peter Clement, Joan Johnston, Katy Munger, Carla Neggers, June Cotner, Jane Roberts, William & Martha Sears.

Member of AAR

Elaine Markson

Elaine Markson Literary Agency, Inc.

She calls herself "a sort of den mother to agents," and indeed that is one of the many roles Elaine Markson has played over the twenty-five years she has been an agent. Her office, like many of her values, seems old-fashioned in the best sense: a genuine Greenwich Village walkup, where the visitor has to mount many stairs to reach her dim, cluttered rooms, decorated with plants, piled bookshelves and a large, comfortable sofa. She is a motherly type, with kind, shrewd eyes behind her glasses and a warm, frank manner.

Her early employment was in the magazine business, working for a time at the Comic Books Association and at *Look* magazine. But she had a family, and to augment her income did some freelance reading for, among others, Knox Burger, then a Fawcett editor. When Burger hung out his shingle as an agent, she joined him (and, she claims, discovered one of his current stars, Martin Cruz Smith, very early in the writer's career). Then, after two years learning the ropes, she went out on her own. The year was 1972, "I'd already done a lot of reading, assessing, and selling, and it was easier to start up then." She has grown up along with big names in the book industry. "Two of my earliest friends in the business were Phyllis Grann, then at McKay [and now, of course, head of Penguin Putnam] and Joni Evans [then at William Morrow, now a high-powered William Morris agent]."

Markson started out, she said, looking for literary people, and some of her earliest clients included Alice Hoffman (who went on to become one of her major sellers), Norma Klein, James Welch, and Andrea Dworkin. "The earliest clients had to come to my bedroom," she jokes. "But although I'm an optimistic person, the business at first just wasn't paying the rent. Even when I was selling books, the money didn't come in fast enough." So, before she could afford her own space, she began to share space with others, with Phoebe Larmore at first (who eventually went off to California), later with Virginia Barber.

Although she had begun on a more literary note, she was also interested in suspense fiction and journalism, and her list gradually began to reflect this increased interest in quality nonfiction: biographers like Donald Spoto and Deirdre Bair, cultural critics like Neil Postman and Neal Gabler, later Jeffrey Masson, Frederick Busch, Paul West, even into some children's literature with Norma Fox Mazer. And with her sturdy anti-Establishment persona (she is very much a child of the sixties) she attracted ardently political feminist writers like Grace Paley and Tillie Olsen.

Unlike some older agents, she makes a point of staying in touch with younger editors. "Some of them feel it's difficult to get to know the golden oldies," she smiles, "but when the younger ones call me for lunch I never say no; I want to see who's coming along, what they're interested in." She even goes still to writers' conferences, and recently found a new client, Billie Letts, at one.

Her list is tilted, about 60-40, toward fiction writers, but she still enjoys "solid investigative journalism," occasionally suggesting a subject to an author, though she's more interested in authors coming up with their own subjects. She actively edits and tries to polish up clients' work: "I got that from Knox." She goes on: "You have to tell writers what doesn't work," recalling that after Alice Hoffman's remarkable first novel, *Property Of...* her second didn't work, and she had to tell her to put it away, write something else, and perhaps return to it later, which she did. She doesn't find anything much among the many unsolicited manuscripts she receives from would-be writers impressed by her client list, but gets most of her new clients out of recommendations from her writers, or from editors. "The problem with material in the slush, is that the things that are just better than the rest, come to look like gold—and the biggest mistake an agent can make is to take something on because they can *probably* sell it, they have to *love* it."

> *"You can't kid yourself that you're now anywhere but in a corporate world, with corporate values. Once you understand that, you can learn to live with it, adjust to it. And you have to persuade your writers, too, that when they're rejected it's not them, it's not the editor, it's some nameless corporate structure and style that's doing the rejecting."*

She is as decisive in her views about present-day publishing, and if they sound at least partly political, so be it. "You have to realize you're totally dealing with corporations now. Even someone like Roger Straus [president of Farrar, Straus & Giroux, a noted literary house] is still part of a corporation, and there are only a handful left that are true independent publishers, like Norton, for instance. So however fine the editors are—and there are still some fine ones—they're still members of a corporation, answerable to people who don't read books or know much about writers. All they're looking for is for their editors to find them new best-sellers, which will always be a gamble."

She remembers other times. "When I went into the business it wasn't like that, but you can't kid yourself that you're now anywhere but in a corporate world, with corporate values. Once you understand that, you can learn to live with it, adjust to it. And you have to persuade your writers, too, that when they're rejected, it's not them, it's not the editor, it's some nameless corporate structure and style that's doing the rejecting. And when they do accept you, it's now Barnes & Noble that's helping to design your cover."

As a result of the corporate stress on increasing profits, "the belief system has changed: editors are now much more frightened of going out on a limb and saying 'I *must* have this book.' They used to be able to convince their bosses of that; if they felt strongly enough, they would have fought for it. Their taste is still there for the good stuff, but they're second-guessed so often that where they once might have fought for a book, they now tend to shy away from things they know are going to be a tougher sell."

Markson, who stresses that she came out of sixties confrontational politics, says she welcomes bargaining and arguing. "What you can get for a book used to be based on what the publishers thought they could get back; now I feel you can often get more than you expect, because the publishers will often write off what they've paid over what the book makes." Still, writers with spotty track records have a credibility problem, which they can overcome by changing their names, as some have, and presenting themselves as first-timers.

What she does find difficult is the declining number of editors now who can balance literary and commercial considerations. "Too many of the older editors who could do so have been fired or let go, and are therefore no longer available to mentor younger ones, who need such guidance."

But despite all the problems, Markson is, as she says of herself, an optimist, one who "really loves books, and thinks they're important, that writers and publishers have a responsibility to art as well as commerce." She adds, "I still love to come to work every day."

WHO: Elaine Markson Literary Agency, Inc.

WHERE: 44 Greenwich Ave.
New York, NY 10011
212-243-8480; fax: 212-691-9014

WHAT: General fiction and nonfiction, mostly literary and quality, 60-40 in favor of fiction.

LIST: About one hundred writers, including Alice Hoffman, Norma Klein, James Welch, Andrea Dworkin, Donald Spoto, Deidre Bair, Neal Postman, Neal Gabler, Frederick Busch, Paul West, Norma Fox Mazer, Grace Paley, Tillie Olsen, Jeffrey Masson.

Jean Naggar

Jean V. Naggar Literary Agency

Everyone, editors and fellow agents alike—to say nothing of her writers—always say how nice Jean Naggar is, and it's a word you would not expect to hear used in connection with someone who has made a number of record-breaking deals for her clients. But it's true. Jean, a rather stout woman with expressive dark eyes, a ready smile and a wonderfully mellifluous voice (born in Egypt to English and Italian parents, she was educated at London University and sounds as if she has never left the old country), exudes warmth and concern. So how has she been able to negotiate such high prices for many of her clients, including first novelists? One of her top and biggest-earning clients, Jean Auel, explains it this way: "She has an iron fist in her velvet glove. She is a tough, tough negotiator, but she handles it all so delicately."

Naggar's path into agenting was more circuitous than most, though she got an early glimpse of it even before she left England. An agent at the David Higham agency placed a poem of hers in *Listener* magazine ("amazing to think an agent would take on an eighteen-year-old with poems!" she marvels now). Later, when her husband was moved to the United States, and she had two small boys in rapid succession, she felt she had to do something to help pay the bills, and "in my innocence thought I'd try for something in publishing." She called everyone she could think of—"I was very nervous, but I phoned and phoned"—and finally got an interview with Gene Young, then a managing editor at Harper & Row. Like everyone else, Young told Jean she needed experience, whereupon Jean (even then hard to shake) said: "Well, you weren't all born in publishing, you had to start somewhere." So Young gave her two books to read, saying one had been a big hit, the other had flopped. Which, and why? Jean wrote reports on both, stating her usual strong opinions, and Young told her she had a feel for it and started her reading unsolicited manuscripts, and doing the occasional French and Italian translation. "It was lots of fun and I loved it."

A third child followed, as did a class at Doubleday in proofreading and copyediting, and the freelance work—reading, translating, editing—continued to pile up. "But I felt very much on the outside looking in; I never got the finished books," Jean complains. She did book reviews, reading for Book of the Month club, "anything I could lay my hands on that enabled me to stay at home with the children." Finally, feeling she could get out of the house, she took an editorial position at Liveright, where six months into the job she signed up two authors who were later to become the nucleus of her list as an agent: Nancy Willard's first book of adult fiction, and poetry by Linda Paston. Jean was made managing editor, and suddenly found herself having to set up systems to make the company work. "I had to find out how everything functioned, how it all hung together. In six months I got a crash course in book publishing." Everything looked rosy, then in 1975 Liveright was suddenly sold to Norton for the sake of its backlist, and its editors were out of a job.

It was a time when a lot of editors were suddenly fired at Macmillan, and the job market was tight; in fact Jean even wrote an article at the time for *Publishers Weekly* on "the job crisis"— and experienced it herself. She ran around for a year, wrote dozens of letters, got no job—but some interest from a publisher in a book that had been let go when Liveright was bought, Janet Bode's ironically titled *Fighting Back*. The author asked Jean to represent her, and she agreed. "I looked at the contract from the author's point of view." Then she called up agent Elaine Markson and asked her about the changes she'd made. "I always knew you'd become an agent," Markson told her approvingly, and sent her author Carol Anshaw, whose book *They Do It All with Mirrors* she promptly sold. Still insisting she really wanted to be an editor, Jean found herself running an agency she called Manuscripts Unlimited with a friend, "and they did indeed come pouring in." Each woman was working out of her apartment, but after a time they agreed to go their separate ways, and Jean was on her own. It was 1978.

At first she continued to work out of her apartment, then rented another tiny apartment as an office; it was so small she kept manuscripts in the unused oven in the kitchenette. She hired a part-time assistant, "and the day we moved into larger quarters, doubling the rent, came word that Nancy Willard had won the Newbery" (an award for children's books that means an automatically much bigger sale). But it was the famous deal for Jean Auel and her series of novels about prehistoric times that really put the Naggar agency on the map. Naggar had met Auel at a writers' conference at Willamette, Oregon (where she lived), but contrary to legend, she did not have the manuscript with her; in fact she sent it to the agent two years after their meeting. Husband Serge read it first, told her: "You've got to read this right away," and "I thought it was the best thing I'd ever read, perfectly presented, complete with maps and a bibliography—a whole new world. I knew it was the sort of opportunity that only comes once." She went at once to three houses that had good publicity, and which she knew needed a big book. There was a three-day auction, with Jean insisting on six figures, and it ended up going to Carole Baron at Crown for the then unprecedented sum for a first novel of $130,000. "It changed both our lives," Naggar says.

But she also says that although people tend to focus on her best-sellers (another major coup was the $360,000 she got from Random's Kate Medina in 1985 for Karleen Koen's *Through a Glass Darkly*), "we sell on an average forty to fifty books a year, including a few children's books, and of course they're not all big best-sellers." Her clients include Mary McGarry Morris (recently an Oprah book club choice, with the resultant surge in sales), Phillip Margolin (whom she represented for ten years before his big breakthrough with *Gone But Not Forgotten,* and who now commands huge advances), Mermer Blakeslee, Carl Safina, Judith Merkle Riley, and Kristin McCloy.

Naggar is regarded among agents as an ace strategist, someone who will think long and hard about where to send a book for the best combination of publisher, editor, and likely promotion, resorting to auction only when she feels several contenders could be of equal merit, which is seldom. "And I'm much more interested in building someone's career, seeing them develop, than simply make a quick flash-in-the pan sale." She seldom takes on a new writer personally these days, though her staff of five do, "and I look at everyone they take on." She estimates the agency receives five thousand to six thousand query letters a year, she personally peruses about three hundred requested and new-client manuscripts, "and the mail has done nothing but increase." Everything that is submitted properly, however, gets read and replied to. She can still get excited by an extraordinary manuscript, but confesses this is quite rare. "Most can't create a unique voice, a way of telling things that speaks to a reader. On the whole, I think too many people today are writing to a kind of formula."

Although she continues to make good sales of previously unknown authors (her list is roughly two-thirds fiction, which is what principally interests her), Naggar is concerned that it's becoming harder to do so.

"Personal passion is what makes books work, and I'm afraid editors are often not allowed personal passion these days," she says. She also feels they are second-guessed too often. "Recently we were asked by an editor for changes in a manuscript, the author made them, then it was given to someone else to read who said they didn't like the voice of the main character. I'm afraid some editors are so afraid of losing their jobs that they don't want to make decisions with any element of risk about them." Another example: "I have an epic historical novel, and showed it to a few people who thought it was a great read, but felt it was too old-fashioned for the public now. But how do they *know* that? Obviously they can't."

"We're sending out too many things that editors say they love but they can't buy. One editor told me recently that no matter what she personally thought of it, she can't buy anything that couldn't be expected to sell between eight thousand and ten thousand copies. But I think five thousand is a great readership for a book, if those readers are people who love the book!"

Editors are also more irresponsible about how long they take to respond—"they assume everything is multiple submission, so there's no rush. And they lose manuscripts and don't seem to care." She notes a particularly irritating anomaly observed by more than one agent: "You get catalogs from a publisher by messenger, but contracts and checks, which you're really panting for, come by surface mail!" She thinks that many houses, as an economy move, are cutting back on office functions, making everything slower, "but there's really no excuse."

Her chief concern in the new climate is the fate of good writers who have not achieved the kind of sales levels publishers are seeking now. "Some good people are going downhill because of past sales records, and that's so short-sighted. You never know when someone is going to write the book that makes it all worthwhile." Publishers' corporate owners, she feels, are loading overhead costs onto them, making it too difficult to make a profit with a reasonable sale. "We're sending out too many things that editors say they love but they can't buy. One editor told me recently that no matter what she personally thought of it, she couldn't buy anything that couldn't be expected to sell between eight thousand and ten thousand copies. But I think five thousand is a great readership for a book, if those readers are people who love the book!"

She shrugs: "I think it will have to get better." But she doesn't sound too sure, and her eyes are troubled.

WHO: Jean V. Naggar Literary Agency

WHERE: 216 East 75th St.
New York, NY 10021
212-794-1082

WHAT: General fiction and nonfiction, about two-thirds fiction, with a higher incidence of first novelists than most. Some children's authors.

LIST: About one hundred active clients, producing forty to fifty books a year. Authors include Jean Auel, Carol Anshaw, Karleen Koen, Philip Margolin, Mary McGarry Morris, Nancy Willard, Mermer Blakeslee, Carl Safina, Judith Merkle Riley, Kristin McCloy, Nancy Springer.

Member of AAR

Richard Pine

Arthur Pine Associates Inc.

There have been a number of agencies in the past that involved more than one generation, but the sole present-day example of a father-son operation with both partners still active seems to be the company run by Arthur Pine (a lovable older figure known affectionately to everyone as Artie) and his son Richard. The face-to-face interview is conducted with Richard, a balding, lean man with an air of coiled energy and watchful intensity; Artie is, for the second year running, wintering in Florida and leaving Richard to mind the store. ("I guess by now he's no longer worried I'll mess it up," Richard says with a grin.)

As the interviewer waits to talk to Richard, he can be heard on the phone, in a long and frank discussion. It turns out to have been a talk urging necessary changes in a manuscript to one of his authors. "You have to get the book in publishable shape before it goes to the publisher," he says, a job he regards as very much his own. "I think I'm a pretty good reader, and I don't hesitate to give my clients helpful criticism of their work," he says. "Times are getting tougher and tougher in terms of the acceptability of manuscripts. The publishers want completely finished books now. They don't have the time to do much editing."

Artie Pine, he explains, started the agency in the early 1960s. He came from a background in publicity, creating campaigns for a number of celebrities, "and thought publishing was an up-and-coming business"; so he gave the promotional business to his brother and became an agent. "He knew a lot of people in show business, especially columnists. He'd go after them, ask them 'Do you want to do a book?'. They wouldn't know how to get started, so he'd write a proposal for them, to get the whole project off the ground." A big break came when Pine saw a newspaper article about a St. John's University professor of psychology named Wayne Dyer giving an evening adult education class on Long Island and wrote to him suggesting he might be interested in writing a book. The result was *Your Erroneous Zones,* originally published without much fanfare by Grossset & Dunlap. Dyer proved, however, to be such an indefatigable salesman and promoter of his own work—he would load the back of his station wagon with copies and insist that bookstores take them on consignment, as he lectured and signed copies—he eventually made his book a huge international best-seller. This was about the time Richard himself formally joined the business. "It was a very exciting time, with Wayne doing so well. He was giving a lot of public speeches, and getting $300 to $400 per appearance. I started representing him as a speaker, and bumped his fee up to $5,000."

Richard's first involvement with the agency was when he was in the eighth grade, and his father handled United States rights for a group of small British publishers. "He'd write submission letters, I would type up multiple copies, pack them up with the books, and take them round on my bike to the post office. If my father sold them, I'd get 10 percent of whatever he made on the deal." Later, when he became more seriously involved, "it was in the mid-seventies, and there was lots of excitement in the industry, and I thought this was the job for me. My father was a well-liked guy, so there was a lot of good-will around, which made it easy for me to get a start." Still, he acknowledges that "for my first five years here, my dirty little secret was just how much I appreciated the faith of any writer who was prepared to be represented by me. I knew little about marketing, branding, or coordinating publicity." And he had one inestimable advantage over many fledgling agents: he didn't have to depend on commissions. "My father always paid me well, so I never had to take on people I didn't want to."

In addition to fiction and journalism, the agency did—and does—well with diet and psychological self-help titles. Dr. Andrew Weil is their latest internationally best-selling author in this field, with *Eight Weeks to Optimum Health,* and other books, and Pine recently closed a deal licensing to Time Warner the material appearing on his very popular Web site. Still, the agency has never really thought of specializing. "It's always been an eclectic list. It was just a little organization that got bigger and bigger." It's still not all that big: there are about 125 active clients, producing between them perhaps twenty-five new hardcover books in a typical year. The proportion is roughly 60-40 in favor of nonfiction. Among the very big sellers in nonfiction was the work of the late centenarian George Burns. "They were a sort of prequel to the celebrity books, like *Seinlanguage* and *Couplehood,* that they're doing today," says Pine. "We'd get the idea for a new book, pitch it to Burns's manager, get an okay in an hour, then give it to Phyllis Grann at Putnam. She'd say yes, and everyone was happy." A number of best-sellers were born that way, right up to the comedian's death. Now the agency is working with television star Carroll O'Connor, who, they hope, has much of the same bond of affection with his audience.

Celebrities are often difficult for publishers to deal with, he says. "They're often not very cooperative, they almost never want to write themselves, so you have to find someone good to write it, and they often expect to get overpaid." And he is scorn-ful of some of the huge sums being paid now. "If you have to pay someone millions, you got to them too late. The thing to do is get to them when they're just cult figures, without huge national publicity, and pay a lot less. You've got to get there first, not when everyone wants them." In any case, the market for older stars such as Burns is pretty much gone now, he thinks.

"Publishers don't spend enough time and money making the most of their successful authors. Since they're going to lose money on 90 percent of the books they publish, why not do better with the 10 percent that do work?"

Other notable names on the agency's roster are Katherine Dunn, Mikhal Gilmore, *New Yorker* writer Susan Orlean, and of course James Patterson, who joined in 1979 but has become a huge best-seller in the past six years. Pine recalls that the thriller author came to them after he read something about the Pines in *Publishers Weekly.* "I think he liked the combination of my father's age and wisdom and my enthusiasm." One of his great ambitions is to secure similar prominence for Peter Blauner, a writer of urban thrillers, who offers tales with a spectacularly closely observed New York setting.

There is no doubt that for all his sometimes hard-boiled attitudes, Pine is a huge enthusiast for the job, for books, and their authors. He may be less accessible to new writers than he once was—"I'm too busy organizing the careers of my existing clients"—but new ones will be added occasionally, usually by recommendation or reputation. To Pine, books are still "sacred texts, and if you never completely forget that, you'll get more from authors and more from publishers."

One of his beefs is that publishers "don't spend enough time or money making the most of their successful authors. The really big ones need the kind of brand-name marketing they usually don't get. Since they're going to lose money on 90 percent of the books they publish, why not do better with the 10 percent that do work?" He also feels that mass market paperback publishing, particularly in backlist books, "which should be the heart of the business, is being let go, and publishers are letting unimaginative retailers call the shots."

As for the future of the agency, he has two young sons, and "I wouldn't warn them against it. It's already been good to two generations of us, financially and emotionally."

WHO: Arthur Pine Associates Inc.
Arthur Pine, Richard Pine

WHERE: 250 West 57th St.
New York, NY 10107
212-265-7330; fax: 212-265-4650

WHAT: General nonfiction and fiction, 60-40 in favor of nonfiction, stressing journalism, self-help, diet, celebrity titles.

LIST: About 125 active clients producing about twenty-five books a year. Authors include James Patterson, Dr. Andrew Weil, Wayne Dyer, Carroll O'Connor, Katherine Dunn, Mikhal Gilmore, Peter Blauner, Susan Orlean.

Aaron Priest and Molly Friedrich

Aaron M. Priest Literary Agency Inc.

The pair are inseparable in the eyes of the publishing world, though Priest's is the name on the door—and he is, the interviewer is astonished to learn, still the agency's sole owner. Though Friedrich has worked with him for twenty of the twenty-five years his agency has been in existence, she is not a partner, and still works essentially on a commission basis—but considering that her clients include Sue Grafton, Frank McCourt, Terry MacMillan, and Jane Smiley, that's not exactly a hardship post. The way Priest describes her role, "Molly is basically a large gorilla; she can do whatever she wants to do."

Interviewing them was complicated because they were both in the room at the same time. Both talk rapidly and excitedly, they interrupt back and forth, agree, disagree and go off on tangents. It's exciting, but wearing to an interviewer, and in order for the interview not to read too much like a play, in chunks of dialogue, their voices have been largely separated so the Priest-Friedrich story can be told roughly in sequence, one person at a time.

It begins, naturally, with Priest, who is an affable man with fashionable glasses and a beard, and who seems perpetually in shirt sleeves. He began, after graduation from Columbia, by working briefly for an insurance company before deciding he wanted to sell something. "Since I'd been reading since I was four years old, and liked books, I thought it might as well be books." So he enrolled in the training program at Doubleday, and spent the next fourteen years as a book salesman, first in upstate New York, then based in Dallas. All this selling experience was valuable for him in two ways: "I got to meet a lot of authors, and hear about their problems, and it gave me a good idea of what people out there in the country beyond New York were interested in reading, and it wasn't always what New York thought it was." The idea of agenting began to seem like a natural, and on his first try he came back to New York, and with Doubleday's approval and letters of introduction, he began to talk to existing agencies. "A lot of the agents then were simply coasting, living on their author estates, and the last thing they wanted was someone who was really interested in selling new authors," puts in Molly. "Yeah, once I began to talk to them I could see why they wouldn't want to hire me, I would probably shake things up too much," Priest agrees. "Of course, I think they made a big mistake."

So he want back to Dallas for a couple more years to save up the money to launch on his own, and did so in 1974. "It was slightly brave but not really heroic," he says. "True, I had a wife and two kids to support, but I had been a good sales rep, so I knew that if it didn't work out I could have been hired in sales in a couple of hours." And at first nothing happened. "For the first six months I didn't sell anything, then in the next fifteen I found I was doing better than I'd hoped to do in five years." The reason was a team he called The Boys, Frank Schaeffer and Terry Newcomb, two advertising writers who'd submitted some manuscripts and film treatments over the transom. He liked their stuff, but didn't feel he could sell it. Since they were willing to try anything, he asked the editors he met what they wanted. One said a plantation novel, and in no time The Boys, working with a copy of *Mandino,* had created one, which Priest sold for $4,000. Another wanted historical romance; another $4,000 sale. Then Leona Nevler at Fawcett decided she would make the plantation novel her lead title, at five hundred thousand copies, and soon he was turning down offers of $750,000 for The Boys' next pseudonymous project.

Around that time Priest got a call from Erma Bombeck, who had known him in his Dallas sales days. She was without an agent and wanted him to represent her, she had an outline for a humor book about life in suburbia. With his nose for the interests of people beyond New York, Priest told her he thought he could get six figures for it (her previous high was $20,000), and did. The book was *The Grass Is Always Greener Over the Septic Tank,* and it launched a highly profitable collaboration that only ended with Bombeck's death in 1996. Priest found that within a few months of starting out he had perhaps one hundred clients, but he soon whittled that down. "You become more successful as you have fewer," he says, and figures he now has no more than "perhaps twenty-three or twenty-four" active clients.

With his growing business, Priest thought he needed help, and remembered a young, energetic publicity assistant at Doubleday. Enter Molly Friedrich, an attractive, highly energetic blonde with a huge smile and a sense of inexorable purposefulness. She studied art history at Barnard, had a formidable family background as the daughter of author Otto Friedrich, and the niece of best-selling art historian Ernst Gombrich. It was in fact Uncle Ernst who told her there were no jobs in publishing for people like her; "find something else to do." But at the time Friedrich was renting a room in Doubleday editor Tom Congdon's house, and he told her the opposite, even got her an interview with the company. "I got minus thirty-seven points on my first typing test," Friedrich says with a laugh. (A typing test was then a requirement for an entry-level job in publishing.) Eventually, however, practice made perfect, and she became the last to be taken on in the publisher's intern program in 1974. She had a choice between becoming secretary to Kate Medina or Loretta Barrett at Anchor, and chose the latter. Eventually she became publicity director there, and since it was the time Doubleday was basking in the *Roots* phenomenon, she found she had to sell very hard indeed to get attention for Anchor's books. "Good training for an agent," she comments wryly. She spent a year with Phyllis Seidel, where she found that her publicity experience was indeed valuable. "I knew what was supposed to happen to get attention for a book, and if it didn't I became a very noisy advocate on behalf of my author."

When she agreed to join Priest, "Aaron made it clear he wanted an assistant and not another agent," she says demurely. "When he left me alone in the New York office while he went off to California to open an office there, I sold three books while he was still on his way. So after that I was allowed to take on my own clients."

She figures she currently has about seventy-five, a figure that draws an amazed exclamation from Priest, with only a third as many: "I didn't realize you had so many, Molly." "Well," she says, "sometimes I just can't resist something that comes in, sometimes it's the person. Sometimes representing someone is a question of ebb and flow, where they have nothing to say, just want to talk." She feels she does best with someone who is coming to her fresh, rather than after being represented by another agent. "Those have to be trained out of their bad habits. Bad dog!" she exclaims delightedly.

Friedrich has her own idiosyncratic working habits. With two children and a new baby, she spends as much time as possible at home, so is in the office only three days a week, though always available by phone. "I could take a whole month away if I wanted to, but your authors always have to know you're there." She is equally flexible about her policies as an agent, sometimes charging 15 percent commission, sometimes 10 percent and in rare instances handling a book for the pleasure of it alone. According to Priest, "Molly saves me a lot of the transom stuff, and in return she doesn't have to be involved in any of the accounting side."

Both concentrate on, and have had their biggest successes with, fiction. Priest has a nose for a commercial novel with wide appeal, whatever the critics may think. Robert James Waller's *Bridges of Madison County,* for instance, began very small, with an initial print run by Warner of fewer than seventeen thousand, and, says Priest, "I've never seen anything sell as fast, and I don't suppose I ever will." The following year Allan Folsom's *The Day After Tomorrow* was sold for $2 million, still a record for a first novel, with Friedrich orchestrating the panic calls while Priest was away on what was supposed to be a vacation in Barbados. David Baldacci (*Absolute Power*) is his most recent blockbuster author. Priest still has a few nonfiction authors—"with nonfiction you can figure out the right combination of author, subject, and marketing, but most nonfiction books you put together like that are basically magazine articles, and it's boring, so I prefer fiction, and I figure what I like, a lot of other people will like too."

"At first you have to concentrate on plot, because that's easiest to sell. Then if you're lucky you can get to go for the characters; at the end you'll go for the final thing, the original voice. When you get all three, it's pay dirt." **(Friedrich)**

Friedrich's first big author was Jane Smiley, whom she acquired for her fourth book, *The Greenlanders,* which, she notes, "coincided with Sonny Mehta's arrival from London to head Knopf." He wanted a big book, and gave the novel a huge promotion, which in turn gave Smiley "a terrific facelift." She began representing Sue Grafton when she was building, in her alphabetical mystery series, toward her current great success. Terry MacMillan, who had a meager $7,500 contract for her next book when she shopped around the manuscript of *Waiting to Exhale,* saw six agents before deciding on Friedrich. "I saw her energy from the start," exclaims Friedrich.

Friedrich has her own sense of the trajectory of an agent's career in regard to what she looks for in a writer. "At first you have to concentrate on plot, because that's easiest to sell. Then if you're lucky you can get to go for the characters; at the end you go for the final thing, the original voice. When you get all three it's pay dirt—but to find all three in equal strength is very rare, hardest of all to find." Friedrich had recently made a notably big sale of a book of short stories, "and what made that sale was the voice." She is modest about her extremely high reputation. "You have to be lucky. An editor told me you have to be right twice, then you get hot and people send you things."

On the ills besetting the book business, both get to have their say.

Priest: "I miss the 'let's do it' spirit you often find outside New York, which means you tend to begin to lose enthusiasm, which is fatal. Editors used to listen better. I recently had three different meetings with a publisher to try to get the books out."

Friedrich: "Sometimes you can have a great campaign, a great book, but you can't get the people into the store to shell out the $25 to buy it."

Priest: "There are certain books on which you want to make a stand..."

Friedrich: "But the numbers are all-dominating. I heard about an editor at Simon & Schuster who said he wouldn't take on a book that was likely to sell less than thirty-five thousand copies. That's crazy; most publishers would love a sale like that."

Priest: "Too many people these days are in over their heads. It's the Peter Principle—they don't have a sufficient grasp of the overall business. And it's much more joyless. The people you're talking to often don't have a sense of the book or the author. They're good at reading computer printouts but they don't have the vision or imagination they once had. But the big bookstore chains are making it much harder for them. I wish the publishers could get together and use their muscle against the chains."

Friedrich: "Yes, it's less fun, but every now and then, when someone like Frank McCourt does so well, it's such a roll, and everyone's happy—a great author, a great book, a great editor, and it all happens just the way it should. People have actually written to me, thanking me for the McCourt book, and that's amazing and gratifying."

Amazing and gratifying—and often moving almost too fast to transcribe—was what the Priest-Friedrich encounter was; but it also was revealing and ultimately exhilarating.

WHO: Aaron M. Priest Literary Agency Inc.
Aaron Priest, Molly Friedrich

WHERE: 708 Third Ave. (23rd flr.)
New York, NY 10017
212-818-0344; fax: 212-573-9417

WHAT: General fiction and nonfiction, about 70-30 in favor of fiction.

LIST: About one hundred clients, including Robert James Waller, Frank McCourt, Jane Smiley, Terry MacMillan, Sue Grafton, Allan Folsom, Erma Bombeck, David Baldacci.

Robin Rue

Writer's House Inc.

Rue is a warm, attractive, and friendly woman with a disarmingly direct gaze and a delightfully antic sense of humor, who is the widow of the late Alan Williams, one of the great editors until he was sidelined by cancer. At the time of the interview she was leading the Anita Diamant agency, whose founder/owner died in 1996, and which does a good amount of front list publishing, though it has a backlist gold mine in the works (and licenses for further works) of the late V.C. Andrews. (As this book was being prepared for press, Rue moved to Writer's House to become an agent there.)

She has had a meticulous grounding in publishing, having worked with such notable names as Saul Cohen and Bill Gross at Dell (in the golden days of Helen Meyer), with Jim Wade at the Dial Press and later at Rawson Associates, and with Charles Sopkin at Seaview Books. She was then, and is now, mostly interested in fiction, though she still recalls with awe how Eleanor Rawson could "do anything with a nonfiction idea." (*The Scarsdale Diet*, a phenomenal bestseller twenty years ago, is the example she likes to remember.)

Rue left publishing just as the big corporations that had been buying into it began to merge hardcover and paperback operations, in the late seventies ("I couldn't stand working for corporations where books had to be manipulated to fit the lists and the market") and for several years supported herself, unusually for an agent, by writing. She wrote six children's books, under the name Nicole Hart, mysteries, and horse books, published by the Silhouette line at Pocket Books: "I still get some royalties from Europe, but it was very hard work." Forced back into steady employment, Rue worked three years for Armitage Watkins at his agency before deciding to join the Diamant operation. "It had a huge backlist; Andrews was the mainstay, but there were also series like the Untouchables, Falconhurst, a lot of magazine editors, Overseas Press Club writers, a number of titles for the romance and Christian markets, diet books, and early gay fiction too. Anita was a very sane woman, and pragmatic too, and she saw the commercial possibilities there very early. She was interested in a book on boxing as an aid to grooming for beauty, for instance, and I thought she was insane, but she was right. I knew she'd let me be free to do what I liked."

There was another kind of chemistry too. "Anita was one of those people who could call the head of a house to make a deal, but she didn't want to be bothered with contracts—whereas I like contracts, though not when they get too lawyerly. It often seems to me that agents want to get things done, while lawyers want to prevent things from getting done."

She likes to think the balance of clients in the agency is about equally divided between fiction and nonfiction, though her associate John Talbot and Rue both like fiction; she herself does all the young adult books. The authors include Andrew Niedeman (*The Devil's Advocate*), Linda Howard, a writer of women's commercial fiction now graduating to big-time hardcover, mystery writer Bartolomew Gill, African-American writer Sharon Wyeth, and even some Western writers.

Rue says: "I guess it's all over the place because I like all kinds of books, just as I like all kinds of food. I know the business well, because I've been everywhere, and I can get through to most houses; the clout of what's on my list that people really need to have can get me past real hurdles. I have good plans for moving authors along, and I like to work with publishers to help them do that—though you can't force them."

Despite her steady, level-headed approach, Rue is not sanguine about many aspects of the business. "It's tough now for a lot of authors, especially mid-list. If a book is good, it won't now necessarily get published, and I always used to think it would. Most of the authors we make the most money on are ones we've had for years. But it's worth trying anything. If you publish with a small press or a university press you get calls from prestigious houses, and then from commercial houses, so it helps to make something move. Sometimes you have to wait for a few books, but if you get enough good reviews, it happens."

"You remember the editors who gave you a courteous turndown, and you give them better consideration as a result. It works the other way too. There are editors now who don't even return phone calls, and obviously they're not going to be my first choice for something good."

V.C. Andrews, as Rue likes to remind herself, was discovered in the slush pile, which was not slighted at Diamant. They usually respond in ten days on unsolicited material, but Rue notes wryly: "These days more people are writing than reading." She still goes to some writers' conferences, where she and Alan were much in demand as speakers.

In dealing with editors and publishers, Rue likes to remember a friend's comment that "The editor's job is to lie about the company to the author, and about the author to the company," and adds: "The agent is the filter between them. What I try to do is keep the author realistic, the publisher nervous." She doesn't like auctions—"They're tiresome and give me an ulcer"—but will do them when she has to.

She sees relationships with editors very much as a matter of reciprocal respect. "You remember the editors who give you a courteous turndown, and you give them better consideration as a result; it works the other way too. There are editors now who don't even return phone calls, and obviously they're not going to be my first choice for something good." She recently had a contract canceled, with the publisher saying "I hope you'll still think of us." She gritted her teeth, "but I couldn't afford not to." When something really outrageous happens, like a terrible publicity release, or no promised ad, "I send a tough letter. It gives them time to think and get back to you without being trapped by an angry phone call. It also puts it in writing, and maybe it's ammunition they can use within the house.

"As I see it, the basis of the relationship is always to keep it possible for someone to take your call the next day."

WHO: Writer's House Inc.
Robin Rue

WHERE: 21 West 26th St.
New York, NY 10010
212-685-2400; fax: 212-685-1781

WHAT: See Writer's House listing on page 248. Rue's new list has not yet become clear.

Member of AAR

Charlotte Sheedy

Charlotte Sheedy Literary Agency Inc.

She is a comforting figure, a cheerful person with fashionably cut gray hair framing a rosy face, and a warm smile. It is easy to imagine what she must mean to the many authors she represents for, more than most, she seems to think of them as her friends, and with a nurturing friend's sense of responsibility toward them. Not long ago she moved into an office at the Sterling Lord agency, where she now has what she calls "a boutique," but which is in effect like an imprint at a publishing house. She has the responsibility to run her operation as a profit-making entity, but she also gets to share in all Lord's back-office services: mail, accounting, computers, and so on. "And every couple of weeks we all get together to report on what's going on—there's a lot of collaboration. I can send them projects and people, and they can do the same with me."

She made the move three years ago out of concern for her family of clients. "I came into my office one Christmas to get the mail, as I usually do, and I suddenly thought: What would happen to my authors if I got sick? My assistants were working to full capacity, and I was tired of never having a vacation. I was just tired of being responsible for running the whole show. So I came in from the cold, and I'm glad I did." And, irony of ironies, in an office just down the corridor, functioning as a freelance editor, is the man who was her boss when she started out in publishing and later made the first big buy of her career from her: Jim Silberman, a veteran of Dial Press, Simon & Schuster, and Little, Brown, to whom she is still close.

It was at Dial, back in the fifties, that she first went to work in publishing, as Silberman's secretary. "It was an extraordinary place to work," she recalls, "where writers actually had a role in publishing." Novelist E.L. Doctorow was one of her bosses during her thirteen years there, she remembers. "Many of us were active politically, too; it was the Vietnam War years, and many publishing people, including me, were involved in the anti-war movement." It was partly out of her sense that "the history we were taught was pretty limited" that she quit her job and went back to school as an undergraduate, to Columbia in 1969. "Helen Meyer, who was one of my mentors, an amazing woman, thought I was being very foolish. But she suggested at least I could do something useful, and do some scouting on campus for authors." She did so, finding books for her old shop and others: one went to Joyce Johnson, then an editor at McGraw-Hill in its trade publishing days, later to become an acclaimed author and a client. It was also during this time that Sheedy sold a book she wrote herself, *The Jewish Woman in America,* to editor Joyce Engelson, who turned into another good friend. Before she completed her thesis there was a moment of frightful self-doubt: "Here I am, a forty-year-old, and I'll be fifty before I get a Ph.D.! Who will hire me?"

She had been keeping herself going for a while with freelance assignments—"people in publishing always look out for each other, and I've had lots of continuing relationships for decades"—but some sort of full-time work was required, and Joyce Johnson suggested she try agenting, since she knew publishing, and a lot of people in the business. "So the very next day I called everyone I knew to tell them what I was going to do, and

I ordered my stationery." Then began a hard time. With hardly any money, and no support services, Sheedy would get up at 6 a.m., deliver manuscripts to publishers' offices by bicycle to save postage, and copy manuscripts herself at do-it-yourself copy shops. "And those lunches and dinners with editors—as you know, the agent never pays!—helped support me." It took her about three years to begin to make any money, and the book that put her on the map was *The Women's Room* by Marilyn French. "It just overwhelmed me; it represented what my life was all about at that time, and those of so many other women too."

Her old boss Jim Silberman, then just launching Summit Books at Simon & Schuster, heard about it, and asked to see it. "He wanted to read it, but I said 'It's not for you.' I really thought a man wouldn't get it. But he insisted, and sent over a messenger anyway, and said he just wanted to read it over the weekend." On Monday an equally overwhelmed Silberman made her an offer; unbelievably, in view of the book's enormous later success, it was initially $7,500, which went up to $10,000. But the year was 1976, and that was fair money for a first novel. Its success changed Sheedy's life, though not as rapidly as French's; when the agent needed to buy her apartment, she was able to borrow the money for a down payment from her author.

The French novel, a big fiction hit, was hardly typical for Sheedy, many of whose books follow her own interests. As a keen gardener, she represents a lot of gardening books. Also among her 250-odd clients are a goodly number of historians. "There's a large list of rather academic titles, and it's interesting to see what's happened to them. At first they all went to university presses, then for a while trade got interested in them, now it's back to university presses again." She wants to represent only books she likes. So there are a lot of books on Jewish subjects, some children's books, all reflecting her tastes. "I think I have a pretty open mind on writers. I never used to have any mysteries until ten years ago, when a mystery writer asked me to represent her, and now I do a few, but only if I like them."

Her assistant Neeti Madan, she says, has taken over some of her authors now, and brought interests of her own into the agency: books of African-American history, pet books—in fact our talk is interrupted by the arrival of an enthusiastic puppy, who wriggles from Madan's arms and runs around the room.

The foreign market is very important to Sheedy, and she used to always go to the Frankfurt book fair, but now finds she can do her foreign deals by employing sub-agents. At first she would prospect for writers at writers' conferences, but now seldom does that either.

Sheedy is not a line-editing kind of agent, and tries not to have to go through several drafts of a book before she feels it is right. "But I will read critically and, especially in the proposal stage, make lots of suggestions; sometimes, if I think a book needs it, I'll suggest a freelance editor."

"The biggest problem is how to cope with a book when an editor leaves the house where he or she bought it. How do you move the book, how do you handle the transition to a new house if necessary? After all, the agent doesn't get paid twice."

Sheedy doesn't chime in with the general chorus of complaint about editors today. "They're so hard-working, so I'm not surprised when they take a while to reply. No, I think the biggest problem I have is how to cope with a book when an editor leaves the house where he or she bought it. How do you move the book, how do you handle the transition to a new house if necessary? After all, the agent doesn't get paid twice. Sometimes it works out better for the author when that happens, sometimes worse." But she does find editors now are unaware of publishing history, of how things work. "I'm always surprised by how they seem to lack a sense we used to have, of belonging to a family, of evolving relationships. But I suppose that's the corporate culture at work."

She has some trenchant observations on shifting tastes. "Novels have changed under the influence of television. They have to begin more dramatically than they used to. It's also affected the way people read; they look for quick takes, can't tolerate the slow bits. And ageism now applies very much to authors. Older ones, say over fifty, tend to lose their audience if they don't keep evolving. In terms of reading tastes, there's now a generational change in ten years rather than thirty, like it used to be. And most markets, like movies and music, are largely controlled by boys' tastes."

She sums up with a cheerful sense of a peg in the right-shaped hole: "I'm not really looking for big blockbusters, although of course it's nice if one comes along."

WHO: Charlotte Sheedy Literary Agency Inc.
Charlotte Sheedy, Neeti Madan

WHERE: 65 Bleecker St. (12th flr.)
New York, NY 10012
212-780-9800; fax: 212-780-0308
email: sheedy@sll.com

WHAT: General nonfiction and fiction, nonfiction predominating, including gardening, history, books on Jewish and African-American subjects, some scholarly works, some children's books.

LIST: About 250 clients, including Marilyn French, Joyce Johnson.

F. Joseph Spieler

The Spieler Agency

The Spieler Agency occupies a particularly unusual location, in one of the duplex studios attached to Carnegie Hall; on the way up a visitor can hear the sound of pianists and sopranos practicing their scales. The little room with the lofty ceiling and a short staircase to what would normally be a sleeping balcony is jammed with piles of manuscripts, computers, and books. Joe Spieler is a ruddy-faced, bluff, and cheerful man of middle age, who swiftly and smilingly outlines what he feels are the ideal qualifications for an agent, as represented by himself: "Someone untrustworthy and sleazy and with a fast tongue."

He began, in fact, as a newspaper and magazine journalist, working for ten years as an editor at the *New York Times,* then spent time as a senior editor at the countercultural *Soho Weekly News.* Some time later, around 1971, he wanted to be a trade book editor "but it didn't work out."

Meanwhile the late John Cushman, who was his agent for his magazine writing, suggested he might become an agent too, a notion he rejected at first. Then an executive at McGraw-Hill told him the same thing. Almost immediately two writers he knew asked him to help them get published, "and I

sold the first two properties I got—astounding beginner's luck."
Spieler adds with a grin: "Of course there were far fewer agents
then." It was a struggle to make the agency work at first. "I boot-
strapped the business, never took out a loan. You have to invent
yourself, and part of the anxiety never goes away. I never had to
count sheep to go to sleep. I would count in my head how much
money the publishers owed me, thinking that one day it would
come in."

---

*"I never had to count sheep to go to sleep. I
would count in my head how much money the
publishers owed me, thinking that one day it
would come in."*

It was probably six years, he says, before he began to feel
assured he would make it. He's still surprised, he says, when he
finds a new client he would like to represent—and most of them
come in by recommendation, especially in areas where he seems
to have built, almost without realizing it, areas of specialization,
like music (opera writer Ethan Mordden, Jan Swafford, author
of well-received biographies of Charles Ives and Brahms, and
editor of the popular *Vintage Guide to Classical Music*); ecology
and the environment (Joe Kane, Marc Reisner, Evan Eisenberg,
former Sierra Club Books director Jon Beckmann); and business
(Paul Hawken, who has brought in others in both cutting-edge
theoretical and practical approaches to that subject). Actor/nov-
elist Peter Coyote is also a client; Spieler has only half-a-dozen
fiction clients among his list of about one hundred writers.

Spieler has four agents: himself, John Thornton, Lisa Ross,
and Victoria Shoemaker, and Thornton, who joins the interview,
is the senior of them. He had bought books from Spieler as an
editor, and had later worked at Book-of-the Month Club. He
joined Spieler about four years ago, at a time when Joe was
thinking he should enlarge the agency to be able to deal with

publishers from a position of greater strength. Now Thornton has put together a series called Vintage Spiritual Classics for Marty Asher, conceived with Walter Laqueur a one-volume encyclopedia of the Holocaust for Yale University Press, and has a growing client list of his own.

Both agents work hard at editing and developmental work, spending a great deal of time getting the proposals right. "If you can get it past me, you can probably get it by any editor," Spieler jokes. Thornton feels they should have a good freelance editor on tap who could take care of a lot of this work, freeing them up for other things. Spieler's beef is the amount of time they spend on the phone—"must be twenty-seven hours a week"—nursing their authors. "They think you have all the time in the world, but it doesn't leave you enough time to talk to editors."

Talking of editors, Spieler feels the relationships have deepened over the years with the ones who have survived. But he also feels there has been a "tightening and narrowing of the appetite for certain kinds of books; the taste out there is not as catholic as it once was, and it's harder now for editors to say they love a book, and that they must have it." Thornton concurs. "Now there's maybe one book in twenty a house will do out of trust in an editor, rather than one in five or six, as it used to be." He adds: "And consolidation seems to produce a division of labor, so that everything has to be signed off on by more people all the time." As for response time, Spieler notes that there are some editors who "always want to get there first." But response times among the others vary enormously, though there seems to be a general rule that "a couple of months means they don't want it."

One area Spieler is especially keen on is foreign sales, which are an increasingly significant portion of the agency's revenues. "You can still sometimes get interest in England before you sell it here, then you can get attention by saying you've already sold it there. I guess they're still allowed quirkier tastes." Thornton adds: "The satisfaction is something like sinking a basket—suddenly to get an unexpected check from a Japanese publisher, years after the sale."

Despite his irritation that Hollywood-style "high concept" seems to count most in the sale of a book—"something you can describe easily in terms of other books"—Joe Spieler says what keeps him going is still "the unalloyed joy of opening a new manuscript by a real writer."

WHO: The Spieler Agency
F. Joseph Spieler, John F. Thornton, Lisa Ross, Victoria Shoemaker

WHERE: 154 West 57th St. (13th flr., rm. 135)
New York, NY 10019
212-757-4439; fax: 212-333-2019
email: spielerlit@aol.com

WHAT: General nonfiction, very little fiction; specialties: music, ecology and environment, business, spirituality.

LIST: About one hundred clients, including Paul Hawken, Ethan Mordden, Jan Swafford, Evan Eisenberg, Joe Kane, Marc Reisner, Jon Beckmann, Peter Coyote.

Philip G. Spitzer

Philip G. Spitzer Literary Agency

Spitzer is an agent who has been through the wars, passing through tougher earlier years than many of his colleagues ever knew, and has finally emerged into prosperity a little dazed and not quite believing in his good fortune.

A pleasant-looking man with a ready smile and warm eyes that nevertheless carry a trace of wariness, he is in fact half French (his father, in law school in Paris, married a Frenchwoman who was part of a "rather raffish" theatrical family), and as a child, right after World War II, Spitzer journeyed regularly between the two countries before settling in New York to complete his education. This included workshops in publishing at the graduate school of the Publishing Institute at New York University, then run by legendary publishing figures John Tebbel and Peter Jennison. Then he was apprenticed for two years, 1961 and 1962, to the New York University Press.

"I loved it—getting paid for working with books, which I've always loved—and I learned a lot and had fun." Then he went back to France for a while, fell in with a group of writers and publishers, further confirming his devotion to the book world. Back in the United States again, he got a sales job at

McGraw-Hill (a few years after the novelist William Styron was a young editor there), and became the sales promotion manager for art books, but after three years felt "there was no place to go." Then a friend ran into John Cushman, at a time when the late agent was just launching the United States office of the big British Curtis Brown agency, and learned he needed an assistant. He reported this to Spitzer, who applied for and got the job.

They were doing literary fiction and nonfiction, mostly by their British clients, which interested Spitzer most, but also category fiction, like gothics and horror, and he found he had a ready aptitude for selling. "I got so I could sell a book by the title alone in those days." Then the agency announced it needed a cutback, "which meant me. I was devastated; I didn't know what to do. A friend at Macmillan asked why I didn't go into business for myself, with my selling skills, but I had three kids to support, and didn't feel confident I could make a living."

That friend, however, knew a printer who owed him a favor, and "for a joke he had a batch of stationery and business cards made up for me, with my name on them as an agent. I couldn't waste them, so I decided I couldn't resist trying it. I wrote to a few people who had been on the old Curtis Brown list, and much to my surprise they said they'd come with me." The year was 1969.

For a while things went reasonably well, and because his wife was working Spitzer felt somewhat secure. "But the kind of books I was doing—some Washington stuff, Ralph Nader's later books (after his big hit *Unsafe at Any Speed*), some serious fiction—didn't backlist well, so there was little royalty income." In 1975 he and his wife split up, and "the Dalton and Walden stores began to come in, the beginning of the modern era of chain bookselling. That didn't help either."

To make ends meet, Spitzer was forced to moonlight, driving a taxicab so he could keep the agency alive. "It was terrible, getting up at dawn, and never knowing who you would pick up." Several times he saw some of the publishers he sold to hailing the cab, he would put up his Off Duty sign and drive away. "One woman got in once, said 'There's a literary agent with your name. How strange!' I thought it was getting too close to home." He confided his plight to an old friend, then Doubleday editor Bill Thompson (who discovered both John Grisham and Stephen King very early in their careers), "he told me not to get too involved in cab driving and, to help, bought a book from me."

It took ten years, but finally in 1985 things began to pick up. "In that one year I had three books published that had been written ten years before." One of them was a naval historical novel that went through three publishers before it finally appeared; one of those publishers was the Naval Institute Press, which shortly afterward became famous for publishing its, and Tom Clancy's, first novel, *The Hunt for Red October*. "Just think; my author's could have been their first." Another was far more important, and in fact became the foundation for Spitzer's current success. It was a book that, he said, had been rejected over one hundred times ("that sounds impossible, but whenever a new editor came to a house, even if it had been rejected there before, I'd try again"). It was later hailed by a reviewer in the *New York Times* as a masterpiece of its kind and became the first big seller of the phenomenon named James Lee Burke: *Lost Get-Back Boogie*. Spitzer finally sold it to Louisiana State University Press, one of the few scholarly presses interested in new and off-beat fiction, "and one of my greatest moments was at the New Orleans book show that year, when their booth displayed a huge banner with Jimmy's book on it.

"That was my first real breakthrough, and Jimmy has stuck with me ever since, though I know there've been plenty of approaches by others." Currently the Grand Master of the Mystery Writers of America, Burke now commands seven-figure deals. Another notable Spitzer client is Andre Dubus, a superb short story writer published for many years by Boston's small David Godine Publisher, but who has recently moved to the bigger time of Knopf. "He was loyal too, was with Godine for twenty years and eight books, but in the end I persuaded him that it would be good for David too if he went to a house with a higher profile." It worked out that way, says Spitzer, with Godine's paperback versions of Dubus's earlier titles getting a sales boost from his greater visibility at Knopf.

Spitzer has between forty and fifty clients, roughly divided 50-50 between fiction and nonfiction, with fiction perhaps having an edge. His particular loves are literary fiction and narrative nonfiction—"though I never see enough of that. You tend to get pigeonholed. Crime fiction has never really been my specialty, though I used to sell Joan Kahn (a famous mystery editor) a lot, because we had similar tastes. But I'd guess that three-fifths of the query letters I get are for crime fiction. But I still get literary mysteries like Jimmy's, make a few huge deals." Other successful Spitzer writers include Michael Connelly (now very much a rising star after *Blood Work*), Richard Neely, former publisher and novelist Sol Stein, and *New York Times* writers Richard Goldstein and Sonny Kleinfeld.

> *"When I read a lot of what's published today, I can't believe it. And lots of stuff I could have published, I now can't. Everything has to be 'big' and 'high concept,' like a movie."*

Spitzer works out of his home in fashionable East Hampton now, and has one assistant who does the books and reads all the unsolicited submissions. He travels into New York, however, nearly every week, for a quick round of lunches and dinners with editors and publishers. "I think I get a lot done in the more concentrated period that's necessary if you don't live there." One of the results he seeks from such encounters is ideas from editors to feed to his journalist clients. "Sometimes I even get ideas for people who aren't my clients!"

But he remembers times when more got done on such occasions. "Those drinking lunches with editors often came up with good ideas," he says, sipping absinthe with his interviewer in a French bar in Chelsea. "Now they're in a hurry to get off to their exercise classes or their aerobics."

So much of what he's learned over the years, Spitzer says, seems meaningless now. "When I read a lot of what's published today, I can't believe it. And lots of stuff I could have published, I now can't. Everything has to be 'big' or 'high concept,' like a movie." He strikes a note of mock despair at the narrow range of knowledge some young editors display, their rapt focus on throwaway popular culture. "If I'd known then what I do now, I'd watch TV—MTV, mostly—for four years rather than go to college." But he's sorry for them too. "It can be frustrating for them; when they want to go with an idea or an author, too often the big chains lower the boom on them."

He even has strangely mixed feelings about his current success. "It's nice to be able to pay the bills, but I wish I'd had more of it sooner, then I wouldn't have had to go through those awfully tough times. But money's really not the driving force in what I do. And it's strange to be doing well, as I am, and at the same time feel depressed at all the good things you can't sell."

A gloomy note is his final thought. "It seems as if publishers are publishing *down* now, almost as if they're saying people won't read a well-written novel any more."

WHO: Philip G. Spitzer Literary Agency

WHERE: 50 Talmage Farm Ln.
East Hampton, NY 11937
516-329-3650; fax: 516-329-3651
email: spitzer516@aol.com

WHAT: General fiction and nonfiction, divided about 50-50.

LIST: About forty-five active clients, including James Lee Burke, Michael Connelly, Andre Dubus, Richard Goldstein, Sonny Kleinfeld, Sol Stein.

Member of AAR

Jimmy Vines

The Vines Agency Inc.

Vines is so comparatively new on the scene that when William Morris agent Robert Gottlieb asked him, early on in his five-year career as an independent agent, how he was going to manage in the current publishing climate, he was able to say, quite truthfully (but unusually) that he'd never known it any other way. He is very much a new kind of agent, thoroughly at home with e-mail, one who has consciously cultivated the younger editors in the business, and who has very decided ideas about how to thrive in the tough contemporary world.

Young, boyishly good-looking, and full of enthusiasm, he shares the interview with William Clark, an old colleague from the time they both worked for Virginia Barber. Later they went their different ways for a time and have now finally combined forces as they had originally hoped. "We used to skip out together and conspire to start our own agency. We wanted to rebuild the model of what an agency could be, to fulfill what we saw as a new role," says Vines. But before they reached the point where they could make that happen, Clark went to work with Owen Laster at the big William Morris agency, "where I was able to get a feel of how a big agency operated, and the ways in which perhaps we could adopt the best of that." Meanwhile, Vines had launched the Vines Agency on his own, working at first out of his East Village apartment because he couldn't afford to rent an office (his present office, on lower Broadway, is in an old loft-style building with tall ceilings and big windows).

Vines says that when he threw his hat in the ring and went out on his own, he received "lots of flowers and welcoming gifts" from people who were glad he had joined the agent ranks, however improbable that may seem. He signed up about thirty clients in his first year or two, finding out about many of them through editors he knew, and ultimately realized, as he says now, "It's not the number of clients that counts, but the number of deals per client." And he adds: "Most of the things we represent now go for larger sums—it couldn't work with a lot of smaller deals."

He and Clark now have about seventy clients each, balanced almost equally between fiction and nonfiction, and, says Vines, "It seems to come in waves; we can both turn quickly from one to the other." They both agree that they will not take on something they don't like, no matter how salable it might seem to be: "If you're not passionate about it, you'll never get results." And they stress that for them, the book deal with the publisher is just the beginning for most of their projects. "There are so many possibilities—movies, television, new media, foreign rights." Their fascination with the possibilities of e-mail include the ways in which it extends their ability to maintain regular touch with their authors "without as much hand-holding and phoning."

As they see it, agenting is very much a matter of finding out what publishers want, and then contriving to supply it to them. Vines recalls his mentor Ginger Barber telling him, when he wanted to send a manuscript to one of the very senior editors, that he should stay in touch with his own generation and wait for them to grow. "It turned out to be very good advice, for people grow with their houses, and most of them are now in key positions." He keeps careful tabs on the editors he's close to, and what they're looking for, "and when their tastes coincide with your own, that's exciting." He's been known to ask an editor: "What's a book that you'd like to buy, but that you haven't seen yet?" According to the response, he can put an experienced journalist to work on creating such a title. His proactivity extends to reading gossip columns in search of someone with something lively to say who might conceivably be turned into an author.

"Publishers hire editors, then don't give them enough discretionary power over what they can spend. Why not allocate them a sum each year, divided however they like, and then see how well it's worked out at the end of the year?"

Some typical authors and projects The Vines Agency is involved with include Stephen Rhodes, whose *Velocity of Money,* says Vines, teaches you a lot about what's going on in a specialized world. "People are looking for value for their money, not just for escapism," he insists. Don Winslow writes literate thrillers, published by Sonny Mehta at Knopf—"He's stylish, but I want to get him a bigger readership." He's doing another thriller with a plankton expert, hoping to come up with a new *Hot Zone.* Vines and Clark represent actress/singer Patti Davis (who is also Ronald and Nancy Reagan's daughter), who's doing a new novel; celebrated rock and roll photographer Michael Stipe; for the past three years the books of, and now the estate of, Terry Southern; soap opera actress Linda Dano, who is doing a book for Putnam; a former Mossad agent, Gerald Westerby, who is doing a book on business secrets for HarperBusiness; a cookbook with the trendy Balthazar restaurant in SoHo; Erica Jong's daughter Molly; the rock group U2 for a book they're working on.

The difficulties of selling today, which have always been there for Vines, include having to show the publishers who the likely readers are—"and you can always reach a deal where you've shown a nervous editor how the book can be sold." He's strongly aware of the enormous power in the marketplace of Barnes & Noble; "I doubt most publishers make an offer now without consulting their chain reps." He recalls Barber being outraged at the caution, the dependence on previous sales figures, and that's only been getting worse. "The only way to sell first fiction today is by the high-concept Hollywood-style approach; if it's a literary writer, you have to be prepared for a big hand-selling job." But it's something on which an agent can easily spend too much time, and in the case of one recent book, "I told the author to find a publicist, and it worked, to the point where what would have been a ten thousand-copy book sold forty thousand. It was expensive for the author, but worth it for what it did to his sales record."

Still, Vines is irritated by the lack at publishing houses now of "people who can make things happen. They hire editors, then don't give them enough discretionary power over what they can spend. Why not allocate them a sum to be spent each year, divided however they like, and then see how well it's worked out at the end of the year?" As to ever-slower payment, he is convinced that is part of a built-in corporate policy for delay. "Even on the days when checks actually arrive, they'll arrange it so they only come after the banks have closed for the day."

He and Clark only do a lot of editorial work on a book "if we like it so much that it just has to be done, otherwise it takes too much time out of your life. And perhaps if it needs too much editing you shouldn't have taken it on in the first place."

WHO: The Vines Agency Inc.
Jimmy Vines, William Clark

WHERE: 648 Broadway (Ste. 901)
New York, NY 10012
212-777-5522; fax: 212-777-5978
email: vinesinc@msn.com

WHAT: General fiction and nonfiction, divided 50-50.

LIST: About 140 clients, half for each, including Stephen
Rhodes, Don Winslow, Patti Davis, Molly Jong, Michael
Stipe, U2, Gerald Westerby, William Monahan, Linda Dano,
Terry Southern estate.

Lois Wallace
Wallace Literary Agency, Inc.

Lois Wallace is one of those formidable agents who manages a group of writers both literary and commercial, making the best possible deals for them with a combination of persistence, intuition, and righteous indignation. She is indisputably tough, and can be brutally frank, but equally indisputable is that she cares passionately about good writing and has an almost wistful admiration for those who practice it. Wallace is in many ways the model of what many people outside the book business imagine an agent to be: she is slender and chic, had a classically elite education and still enjoys a tony location (respectively, The Brearley School, Vassar, and an old townhouse on the Upper East Side for offices), smokes like a chimney, drinks at her desk, and has a fund of great anecdotes, most of them offering a refreshing degree of cynicism and a frequently self-deprecating and only occasionally unkind sense of fun.

Almost alone among the agents interviewed for this book, she offered a serious drink to the interviewer, sending her assistant down to a basement refrigerator for ice and a large bottle of vodka, while she sipped Sancerre. She fussed for a while trying to turn off her computer (having finally given in to use of the machine two years ago although the agency still uses color-coded cards to keep track of submissions and contracts, she still seems uneasy with its functions), then turned her attention to matters in hand. "You should have been here earlier, to hear me talking to a client about the reserve for returns, and what it means," she says in her throaty voice. "Seems to me that's something I've been doing ever since I started working for Dorothy Olding at Harold Ober as a secretary in 1962."

That was her introduction to the agent's life, after a brief apprenticeship at publisher G.P. Putnam's Sons, and she remembers it with nostalgia. In her five years there she did everything for Olding, "even handled J.D. Salinger's fan mail, and once I even got to shake the great man's hand." She was surprised by the silly side of the job, however, like "someone who phoned to ask where she could find Seymour Glass's poems, and I think I failed to convince her they weren't real, that Glass was a made-up character." But she liked the people at Harold Ober, and when the time came that she was asked if she would like to join the William Morris agency, she demurred at first. "I thought someday Ober would make me an agent. Then someone asked me if I'd put page numbers on a manuscript, and I thought 'I don't need this,' and went to see Helen Strauss at Morris anyway." When she reported the Morris overture, Olding said she had always intended to make Wallace an agent, but added "I would be uncomfortable thinking you wanted to move into my office." That decided Wallace, and she left.

When she went to work at William Morris, there were some embarrassments. "Agents started having me send out really hopeless manuscripts from friends and relatives, I began by sending them with letters that said without enthusiasm 'I have been asked to send you this,' but then that got too embarrassing as well, so I made up rejection letters so I didn't have to submit them at all." Then there was the show business side of things, that included meeting with "people from the West Coast office who said things like 'look at "properties" with diverging eyes'; books, not as books but as potential movies or television shows." There were clients like Pearl Bailey and Joan Crawford ("I once had to sit and watch her having a pedicure at 9 a.m., and she didn't even offer me coffee!"). But the agency had some notable literary clients too, and it was there she got to represent Joan Didion ("She'd only written one book then, and at our first meeting, lunch at the Plaza, we were both very nervous; I represented her for a long time, for the best of her work, I think") and Joanne Greenberg (*I Never Promised You a Rose Garden*).

There are lightning snapshots of life at the big agency. At first she worked for Harvey Ginsberg, who once asked incredulously, after she had recommended a book, "Did you really go to Vassar?" "That was the first time I was ever in tears, and one of the last." Helen Strauss, her boss, sent in her secretary every day at four to collect her carbons "to see what kind of letters we'd been writing." The only other agent on the literary side was Owen Laster, "but he had come from the television side and knew nothing about books. When they were going to make him head of the literary side, I complained I knew much more about publishing, so they made us co-heads. They wanted us to have regular meetings, but we couldn't stand them, so we would make up the minutes."

Other notable authors acquired at Morris included Don DeLillo, R.K. Narayan, and William F. Buckley, Jr. One of her most spectacular exploits was with Erich Segal, "He hadn't known the agency had a literary department before I wrote to him. Erich sent me some Roman translations," she said of the Yale classics professor's prime interest, "which I sold to Harper & Row." Later he gave her a copy of a screenplay he had written that his movie agents were reading. "They told him to shelve it, which he did, and said 'No' when I urged him to turn it into a novel." Then when a producer optioned the script Wallace asked him again to write it as a novel. " 'If it'll help the movie,' " he said. Wallace sold it to Gene Young at Harper for $7,500; it went on to become a huge bestseller, and, of course, a highly popular movie.

An earlier milestone in Wallace's life came when, on a vacation trip to London, she was asked to sound out English agents to act for William Morris in Britain. She interviewed a number of them and chose Anthony Sheil Associates. They represented the Morris list for years, then in 1974 Sheil and Gillon Aitken came to New York to ask Wallace to set up an American agency, Wallace, Aitken & Sheil. An interesting footnote to agency history. "Whereas Morris had a rule that you couldn't go after the clients of a smaller agency, Gillon Aitken had no such compunction," Wallace says. "He actually had a list of people he wanted to steal. So it was he, rather than Andrew Wylie, who really began the practice." (A further footnote: The late Scott Meredith had been a dedicated poacher years earlier—and Aitken later went to work for Wylie, an agent who because of his predatory ways has become widely known as The Jackal.)

After Aitken moved on, everything worked well for Wallace and Sheil: "We were small and very good." Then Sheil wanted to expand and add more agents in England, while Wallace felt it was becoming harder and harder to sell the British agents' so-so clients in this country. "The good ones, though, were a pleasure: John Fowles, John Keegan, Patrick Leigh Fermor, Fay Weldon." Many of her authors had been her clients at William Morris, "and Owen (Laster) was enormously helpful in convincing the powers there to let them go, although after Erich Segal did they sued him, and threatened to sue me, for 'Inducement to Breach,' which sounded more like a gynecological matter than a legal one."

Wallace's husband Tom, who had long been a senior editor at several houses, including Putnam (where he met Wallace), Holt, where he became editor-in-chief, and Norton, joined Wallace & Sheil as its third agent in 1987. When Irene Skolnick, who has been handling many of the English authors, left next year, Wallace decided against hiring someone else to take them over, and after what she calls "nine months of legal hassle" broke up with Sheil. The agency became simply the Wallace Literary

Agency. (It is still, as of 1998, but Tom has now left to go off on his own.)

Although Wallace mostly reads novels for pleasure, fewer than half the authors she represents write only fiction. "That most of the fiction I represent is fiction I would read no matter what I did is one of the reasons why, after more than thirty years, I love being an agent. Can you imagine how I felt after I'd finished *Underworld?*" Don DeLillo became Wallace's client just before his first novel, *Americana,* in 1971. He'd been recommended, as are most of her clients, by an editor then at Viking who is now a novelist and also a client, Ann Arensberg. She can think of only one client she has *asked* to represent: William Least Heat Moon, of *Blue Highways* fame, after she'd been sent the manuscript by editor Lydia Galton at Little, Brown. Wallace thought she was doing her a favor because Moon didn't have an agent; it turned out that Galton had wanted her to talk the book up, not to represent him.

"A lot of authors are simply not being well represented. You have to know what's reasonable, what you can get out of a publisher and what you can't, or shouldn't, and you have to know contracts, and too many people now practicing just don't."

Wallace's problems today are not so much with editors ("there are still plenty of wonderful ones around, though they don't get to call the shots any more") but with the proliferation of agents. "A lot of authors are simply not being well represented. You have to know what's reasonable, what you can get out of a publisher and what you can't, or shouldn't, and you have to know contracts, and too many people practicing now just don't." And at the other end of the process, the publishers' contracts departments are, she finds, understaffed and therefore much slower than they used to be—though some are better than others; high marks to Norton and Simon & Schuster, for instance.

Yes, of course, selling, particularly of more literary authors, is harder than it used to be. "No one wants to publish something that's going to sell only six thousand or seven thousand copies, and even if they do a great job and manage to sell twelve thousand, the author's still unhappy." Too much knowledge can also be a self-defeating thing. "They never used to ask about previous sales figures, but now they just know, because they have them all at their fingertips, and they're just governed by them. Now editors have to go through department after department, getting lots of approvals, before they can come up with the money."

But despite the drawbacks Wallace says that "I truly love being involved with wonderful writers; what could be better for someone who discovered, very early in life, that there's more to books than just their stories?"

WHO: Wallace Literary Agency, Inc.

WHERE: 177 East 70th St.
New York, NY 10021
212-570-9090; fax: 212-772-8979

WHAT: General fiction and nonfiction, slight edge for nonfiction.

LIST: About one hundred clients doing fifty to sixty books a year. They include Don DeLillo, Marge Piercy, William F. Buckley, R.K. Narayan, William Least Heat Moon, Bruce Fierstein, Ben Stein, Erich Segal, Peter Manso, Ann Arensberg.

Member of AAR

Wendy Weil

The Wendy Weil Agency, Inc.

Wendy Weil is a rather rare bird among agents: she had actually been extensively interviewed, in the journal of the organization Poets & Writers, before sitting for her portrait in this book. And the result had been rather unnerving. For one thing, the time that had elapsed between the actual interview and its appearance in the journal's pages was so long—nearly two years—that some of what she'd said, particularly about several of her authors, had been overtaken by events. For another, it secured her a great deal of not-always-welcome attention from unpublished authors shopping for an agent. "It is immensely time-consuming. First, they call to get my address," she says. "Then they send things by forms of mail that require a signature. Then a day or two later they call to find out why you haven't read it yet."

There is no malice in her observations, however, only a wryly humorous resignation. For Weil, as her previous interview appropriately noted, is nothing if not ladylike in deportment. She is a tall, willowy woman with a rather languid manner and a way of pausing reflectively before replying to a question that instantly slows discourse to a more leisurely pace than is customary in staccato New York. She seems, in fact, to have emerged from a more graceful, relaxed culture, though she is in fact a New Yorker born and bred, who grew up in the city, and made one of her oldest friends, fellow agent Lois Wallace of the Wallace Agency, while they were fellow students at Hunter Elementary, a school for spectacularly bright urban children. (She shows a photo of the two young girls sitting together in someone's garden at least forty years ago.) The two went on to private schools (Friends Seminary for Weil, followed by Wellesley), and finally celebrated together the simultaneous acquiring of their first publishing jobs: Weil in the training program at Doubleday, Wallace at G.P. Putnam's Sons.

At Doubleday Weil worked for noted editor Timothy Seldes, then moved with him to New American Library. At one time she thought she might be interested in working as an editor in children's books, and since agent Phyllis Jackson, who represented Dr. Seuss, had offices in the same building, she went upstairs to ask her about it. Jackson sent her to see the celebrated children's editor Margaret McElderry, but Weil, unwilling to start again as a secretary after recently becoming an assistant editor, decided against it. Fortunately, Mrs. Jackson then offered her a job as a fledgling agent at what was then—in the mid-sixties—the Ashley Famous Agency. It was full of notable, later legendary, figures; in addition to Jackson herself there was Roberta Pryor ("although I'd already been in publishing six years, Roberta taught me a great deal"), Monica McCall, later Lynn Nesbit. Weil fondly remembers the formidable Jackson, who sat at a vast marble desk with nothing on it but a datebook with meticulous details of all her deals. Favored editors would be invited to visit her, to learn what she had on offer.

Soon Weil began to acquire on her own: Judith Rossner (*Looking for Mr. Goodbar*) was one of her earliest clients, as was Jim Magnuson, and Susan Brownmiller, who later moved elsewhere. But after three years Marvin Josephson bought the agency and took it public as what became International Creative Management (ICM). "They cut back on jobs, and I was in shock." Relief was at hand, however: Mary Clemmey, at the Julian Bach Agency, was leaving to return to London, and Weil replaced her. She stayed with Julian Bach for twenty years— "nineteen of them very happy ones," she says, before they parted ways when he sold his company to International Management Group in 1991. Five years earlier, however, she had incorporated on her own. She had also made an arrangement with Bach for the transfer of her clients, and when his sale came, was able to move her list of authors to her new office, "so it worked out fine in the end."

She has now been in business entirely as an independent for seven years, and since she also retained her invaluable bookkeeper and office manager Ann Torrago, "It wasn't as if I was starting a new agency at all." Hers is essentially a one-agent operation, with support from Torrago, an assistant, and interns.

Her list is split about 50-50 between fiction and nonfiction, "though there seems to be a lot of fiction at the moment," and in the year preceding the interview, several of her fiction clients had enjoyed stellar success: Andrea Barrett won a National Book Award, A.J. Verdelle a PEN/Faulkner, and Joseph Skibell had become a strong seller after a set of reviews to die for. "In fact, it's been my best year ever." That's quite a statement coming from one who numbers among her clients authors of the stature of Alice Walker, Rita Mae Brown, the late Paul Monette (another NBA-winner), Fannie Flagg, and Jane Brody (yes, authoritative diet and nutrition books are one of Weil's specialties in nonfiction). She inherited the culture critic Greil Marcus from Mary Clemmey, and represented the spy author Robert Littell (who lived in the south of France and later moved all his representation to his English agent, Ed Victor). No, she doesn't "spirit away" other agents' authors, and feels clients will not change agents "unless they are ready for a move. And if they are, there's nothing you can do to hold them, nor should you try."

Weil seems to have kept alive a powerful enthusiasm for good writing, and rejoices that it continues to surface as often as

it does. Not long ago her assistant Emily Forland found "a startling, original voice—you can't *believe* how good!"—among the
manuscripts submitted as a result of the Poets & Writers interview: *Mother of Pearl* by Melinda Haynes, which will be published by Martha Levin at Hyperion in 1999. She is always
looking out for imagination, intense characters passionately presented, and a freshness of vision. She is happy that since that
interview, in the course of which she regretted having few
thrillers or suspense novels, she has acquired two great suspense
authors, Douglas Kennedy (*The Big Picture*) and Alice Blanchard.

---

*"It's a fine time in publishing for people who
are beginning and really talented. But I'm afraid
it's a mistake to take on people who are just
okay, and publishable, unless you're really excited about their work. It just won't work out in
the end, and you're not doing anyone any
favor."*

She is aware that in many ways writers in mid-career of the
kind she most admires are an endangered species these days.
"There are many writers out there who are suffering because
they've been published in the past with modest sales, and publishers are afraid the stores won't stock their books." She is dis-
mayed, too, by the attrition in the ranks of editors to whom she
used to submit (and many of whom were once her colleagues).
"So many of the editors in my generation quit because they
couldn't do the intelligent books they wanted to do, and didn't
want to acquire the mass market books the marketplace seemed
to be demanding." There is some hope, however: "Today, with
the growing success of trade paperbacks and the emergence of
reading groups, publishers are again buying more literary
books."

She feels that all editors and agents are in search of strong narrative nonfiction, of the kind (*Into Thin Air, The Perfect Storm, Midnight in the Garden of Good and Evil*) that have scored heavily in recent seasons. Such books, she thinks, have done particularly well because of the strong marketing and promotional push behind them.

As to the rest of the current scene, "it's fascinating how the real decision-making is still in a comparatively limited number of hands." She finds the rate of response among publishers to be "both slower and faster, all at the same time. There's terrific pressure on editors to supply same-day or next-day readings on something that's really hot. They're expected to respond literally overnight, which means that in some cases you can get very fast action indeed. But it also means that with more regular submissions, where there seems to be no special urgency, it can take much longer than it used to get a reply."

About the speed of payment there are no such ambiguities. "Contracts and payments are both terribly slow. The publishers are hanging on to the money as long as they can, while the poor authors have bills to pay."

Weil has always gone to writers' conferences—though she often finds she makes more connections there among the faculty, editors, and fellow agents, than among the writers who attend. Still, she did meet Andrea Barrett at Breadloaf. "Once I made a speech at one of those conferences, and told it like it really is for writers, and someone later said that people were crying in the halls afterward," she recalls with a mixture of compunction and bemusement.

She thinks for a while, as she usually does, before offering her summary of the current prospects for writers. "It's a fine time in publishing for people who are beginning, and really talented. But I'm afraid it's a mistake sometimes to take on people who are just okay, and publishable, unless you're really excited about their work. It just won't work out in the end, and you're not doing anyone any favor."

WHO: The Wendy Weil Agency, Inc.

WHERE: 232 Madison Ave. (Ste. 1300)
New York, NY 10016
212-685-0030; fax: 212-685-0765
email: wendyweil@msn.com

WHAT: General fiction and nonfiction, divided roughly
50-50.

LIST: About seventy-five clients, including Alice Walker,
Andrea Barrett, Judith Rossner, Joseph Skibell, Fannie
Flagg, Rita Mae Brown, Jane Brody, Greil Marcus, Douglas
Kennedy, Alice Blanchard.

Phyllis Westberg
Harold Ober Associates Inc.

Harold Ober Associates is a long-established agency that made its big mark forty or fifty years ago, back in the days when magazine sales were an important part of an agency's job. Phyllis Westberg, an auburn-haired woman with a ready smile and a leisurely style that seems pleasantly old-fashioned, now runs it as its president and majority shareholder. The week she sits for her interview, in the agency's spacious, sunny offices on Madison Avenue that it has occupied longer, she thinks, than any agency has been continuously in operation in the same quarters, she is much excited because Emma Sweeney, a bright young independent agent, has just joined Ober, and, she feels sure, will give it new vibrancy.

Westberg herself began in the magazine business, in the fiction department of the old *McCall's Magazine,* reading the slush pile, mostly short stories ("The best possible beginner's job!" she exclaims). Then she worked for a time for one of the Dell magazines, *Horoscope,* and at World Publishing when it had a trade list. She has been at Ober since 1969. At that time the clients were mostly writers for the magazines, or the book authors of Dorothy Olding (another legendary name in agentry) and Ivan von

Auw. Even then, says Westberg, the importance of magazines was beginning to fade, and with colleague Claire Smith, she began to build a list of mostly fiction—"all kinds, including literary." One notable name who came in then was a woman with a friend who rented an apartment from Von Auw; she asked her friend to recommend a literary agent, and that was how Danielle Steel came to them; "yes, she was mid-list too, then," says Westberg with a laugh.

"Too many people just say automatically 'too mid-list' when they mean they didn't bother to read it."

Like some of the other old-established agencies, Ober is particularly strong in estates; in this case those of such classic mystery writers as Agatha Christie, Ngaio Marsh, and Ross Macdonald, and also of F. Scott Fitzgerald. Until recently, thinks Westberg, the list was 75 percent fiction, but is now moving closer to leveling up with nonfiction. Some of the authors who were big in the 1970s, especially in women's fiction and historical novels, are now much more difficult to sell, she says, though she wonders aloud how carefully they are looked at. "Too many people just say automatically 'Too mid-list' when they mean they didn't bother to read it," she notes. Back in the seventies, too, there were more revenue possibilities: "The sub rights department was king—everything went into paperback or into book clubs." Although she agrees that book club buys don't always make a huge difference financially, "they make a difference psychologically; being chosen cheers up the authors and the sales force."

She is succinct about the problems with publishers today: "There are three difficult areas, and they're getting worse: getting answers, getting a contract, and getting paid," she declares. "I guess, despite the computers, there's just too much paperwork for people to handle." And she reveals that she made a deal with Penguin Putnam last May, "and only got a contract last week" (the interview took place five months later).

She also finds, wistfully, that she doesn't have as many lunches with editors as she used to, and they are more fiercely focused on books they are sure can be marketed. "I remember once selling a cat book to an editor just because she liked cats. You don't find that any more." And not long ago she lost a deal because, she sniffs, "they said the author wasn't telegenic."

She likes good mystery writers, and has a couple in Stephen Dobyns, whose light-hearted comic mysteries, many of them set in Saratoga, have developed a strong following, and John Dunning, who writes mysteries with an antiquarian books background and who is, after twenty years finally breaking through. Ober represents the big London agency David Higham in the United States, "so we get a lot of biographies, but that's a problem too, because you suddenly get editors who used to do them saying 'I'm not allowed to do any more biographies.' "

They have been an agency for some notable political memoirs in the past, of people like Adlai Stevenson and Dean Acheson, "but now all people want is celebrity bios, and I don't find those a wonderful experience. You can forget about working with actors and actresses!"

Yes, the agency it still open to taking on new authors, but Westberg herself is too busy with administrative work to actively pursue them, though she does read some of the proposal letters that come in. "They sometimes have great ideas, but the problem is they just don't know how to present them."

WHO: Harold Ober Associates Inc.
Phyllis Westberg, Emma Sweeney

WHERE: 425 Madison Ave.
New York, NY 10017
212-759-8600; fax: 212-759-9428

WHAT: General fiction and nonfiction, now about 60-40
in favor of fiction. Strong in biography.

LIST: Many estates, including Ngaio Marsh, Agatha
Christie, Ross Macdonald, F. Scott Fitzgerald. Current
clients include Stephen Dobyns, John Dunning.

Member of AAR

Al Zuckerman
Writer's House Inc.

Writer's House is just that—a Manhattan town-house, first built as a private bank for the Astor family, and now located rather improbably in an area full of Korean importers' showrooms. It's just off Broadway in the twenties, and it is where the head of the agency, Albert Zuckerman, once lived; it is now filled with agents' offices, on three floors and an extra floor he had to add on as the agency expanded. There are now eleven agents there, plus support staff, and if it isn't the size of William Morris or ICM, it's certainly one of the biggest of the independents.

Zuckerman, who looks a bit like an aging Hollywood leading man, with his iron-gray hair, mustache, and regular features, is one of the few agents who actually began as an author. "I think of myself as a failed writer," he says genially, "or at least as someone who would never be an extraordinary one—but who knows how it should be done." In his younger days he wrote plays, some of which won prizes, published two novels "which made absolutely no money," and wrote three television soap operas which did make money—sufficient to keep him living in decent style for a while. During the time he was writing, nearly twenty years, he had three different agents of his own, an experience that convinced him that "I could help a writer more than any of them had helped me." For a while he taught at Yale Drama School, ran playwriting seminars, and eventually wrote a book, one he is still glad to claim. Called *Writing the Blockbuster Novel,* it is published in six languages, sells extremely well, and has brought him, says Zuckerman, a number of clients and even letters from two authors who claim his advice helped them write million-dollar books.

"Every agent should write a book and try to get it published, just to see what it's like."

It is advice hard come by. One of the agent's proudest possessions, on the mantel in his office, are six leather-bound volumes of his editorial suggestions and emendations on the first-draft manuscript of Ken Follett's best-selling novel of a decade ago, *The Pillars of the Earth.* It was presented to him, says Zuckerman, by Follett himself, whose work he has represented ever since his first hit *The Eye of the Needle,* and who is still, after more than twenty-five years, perhaps his most successful client. Zuckerman is one of the most interventionist of agents, in terms of the time and effort he spends on what he calls "developmental" work. There are a lot of suggestions, revisions, reorderings, rewritings before some of his manuscripts are offered to publishers, and sometimes, he says, the work even continues after they have been sold.

Zuckerman started Writer's House in 1973 on a part-time basis, thinking he would represent mostly plays, television scripts, and movies: "That was what I knew about." But he soon realized that he knew people in publishing from his own brief novel-writing experience and that it was easier to handle books—especially then, at a time when publishers were hungry for new titles. His earliest "office" was in a bank lobby in the CBS building. "I would meet publishers and authors in the lobby, we'd sit on the

bank sofas and chat, and I'd pretend any empty desk was mine."
His first real office was over a porn parlor, a room that also served
as a mail drop. "There was just room for two people; if anyone
else came in they had to stand in the open doorway." He looks
around, bemused, at the fine cherry wood fittings and solid
Victorian furnishings of his current offices, filled with ringing
phones and clicking computers, and says half to himself:
"Difficult to imagine we've come such a long way."

His first-ever sale was a stamp-collecting guide to Europe by
a former high school classmate, and the first good-sized deal set
a pattern of manuscript doctoring he would continue to follow.
It was a book written by a friend in advertising based on an idea
given him by Zuckerman, a multi-character disaster thriller.
After an unsuccessful run at mass market houses it was bought
for $5,000 by Putnam and then just sat there on someone's desk,
untouched. "So I took it back and did a big doctoring job on
it," following which it made its mass market sale after all—to
Bantam (one of the houses that had originally rejected it) for
$100,000, a very decent sum twenty-five years ago. A book sold
to New American Library was followed by a quarter-million
dollar contract for two more. Then in 1977 came *Eye of the
Needle* by the aforementioned Ken Follett. There has been a lot
of controversy over who did what to this book, with both its
publisher, the late Don Fine, and Zuckerman mentioned as having virtually rewritten it from its original version as submitted
by Follett. According to Zuckerman, the only character who
counted in the original story was the spy; on his advice, the girl
and her husband became involved in a major way; "I helped
transform it from a one-character story into a three-character
one, but I did no work on the text itself." Another coup was the
$850,000 Zuckerman extracted from New American Library in
1983 for Anne Tolstoi Wallach's *Women's Work,* at that time the
highest advance ever paid for a first novel. A more recent splash
with another first novel was *The First Wives Club* by Olivia
Goldsmith.

Zuckerman has a larger staff than most independents, and is at pains to point out their particular strengths and areas of interest. Amy Berkower, who started in 1977 as an assistant and receptionist and is now his full partner in the firm, began as an agent by exploring the world of children's books, about which she knew nothing, but Zuckerman told her "You can learn." She is now, he says, the top agent in the field, with such multi-million-selling clients as Ann M. Martin, with her bestselling Baby-Sitters Club series, Francine Pascal, with her Sweet Valley High titles, Paula Danziger, James Howe, and many others. She is also the agent for top women's novelists Nora Roberts and Barbara Delinsky. Berkower, according to Zuckerman, "has more of a business mind than I do; she's a genius at working out contracts, making deals. She's also younger than I am, by twenty years, and she'll take the firm over one of these days when I'm too feeble to go on."

Merilee Heifetz also began as an assistant, then began to specialize in science fiction and fantasy, in which she is now a leading agent, representing such stars as Bruce Sterling, Neil Gaiman, and James Morrow. She also does books on rock and popular culture, and recently began representing songwriter and singer Rosanne Cash as an author. Susan Cohen specializes in children's writers and illustrators, with such people as Mem Fox and Kathryn Hewitt. Robin Rue, former head of the Anita Diamant agency, joined recently as a generalist, with best-selling clients V.C. Andrews and Linda Howard. Susan Ginsburg, former editor-in-chief at Atheneum, does many cookbooks, including the work of Lora Brody, along with romance, popular medicine, psychology, and true crime. Fran Lebowitz (no relation to the writer and gal-about-town) is big in young adult titles and movie tie-ins, works from Singapore via e-mail. Michele Rubin handles domestic sub rights for a number of publishers, has a list that tends to the more serious nonfiction titles. Karen Solem, with a background as editor-in-chief at Silhouette, has nearly fifty romance writers, but also handles some mysteries, and some titles in women's health. Jennifer Lyons, daughter of publisher Nick Lyons, is the foreign-language expert, representing six German publishers (a legacy of the Joan Daves agency, which Writers House absorbed some years ago), also reps some Dutch writers, and is the United States agent for the Japan Foreign Rights Center. New agents representing young cutting-edge writers are John Hodgeman and Simon Lipskar.

How does the agency's huge list—it represents a total of about five hundred active clients, and some estates—balance out? There is probably a bit more fiction than nonfiction, but Zuckerman says that although he personally does more nonfiction titles, "you tend to make more from the big fiction authors." The only two nonfiction clients he sees as really major money-makers are Stephen Hawking, whose *A Brief History of Time* and its spin-offs and sequels became a worldwide publishing phenomenon, and Michael Lewis, whose Wall Street expose, *Liar's Poker,* was also a global success. He finds he sells a lot of small nonfiction books (advances of $30,000 or less) that no longer earn out, but at those levels publishers will at least still take chances. What he calls "small novels," selling for perhaps $15,000–$20,000, are more and more difficult to place.

The major problem facing publishing, as Zuckerman sees it, is how to make the public aware of "a book that is wonderful— or even that it exists." Although publishers still talk about cutting back their lists, bookstores are still flooded with more books than they can handle; meanwhile people who used to spend more time reading newspapers, including their book reviews, no longer do so. "It's not the fault of authors or agents—it's just the way society's evolving." Some areas, like male action, are particularly difficult: "The people who used to buy those titles now use their leisure to play computer games." Still, he sees hope in the interest of foreign readers in United States titles; there are always new overseas markets, particularly, these days, in Eastern Europe.

Zuckerman says he personally receives fifteen or twenty unsolicited manuscripts or proposals a day. Everything is looked at, "and several times a year we'll find something to pick up on and sell." About three-quarters of Writer's House clients, he reckons, have moved there from elsewhere or have been recommended, either by fellow writers or by editors at publishing houses. "I think a lot of them come because they know we have the ability to help talented writers improve their work." This is something he constantly stresses, even urging his staff to try writing novels themselves. "Every agent should write a book and try to get it published, just to see what it's like."

WHO: Writer's House Inc.
Albert Zuckerman, Amy Berkower, Merilee Heifetz, Susan Cohen, Robin Rue, Jennifer Lyons

WHERE: 21 West 26th St.
New York, NY 10010
212-685-2400; fax: 212-685-1781

WHAT: General fiction and nonfiction, with slight edge to fiction. Many specialties, including children's, romance, and fantasy fiction, popular culture, cookbooks.

LIST: About five hundred clients in many genres. Authors include Ken Follett, Michael Lewis, Stephen Hawking, Ann M. Martin, Francine Pascal, Paula Danziger, Mem Fox, Nora Roberts, Barbara Delinsky, Bruce Sterling, Rosanne Cash, Linda Howard.

Member of AAR

Other Agents to Try

The following twenty-one agents, although they were not interviewed for this book, have been mentioned by a number of editors and fellow agents as being receptive and good to work with, and are here listed alphabetically. It should be remembered, when using this book, that exclusion from mention in it means nothing beyond the fact that, among the hundreds of agents currently practicing, those included were ones who had achieved a higher than average degree of notice in the business. As mentioned in the introduction, there were a number who chose, for whatever reason, not to be interviewed or included. For a truly comprehensive listing, see the *Literary Marketplace,* published by R.R. Bowker.

Betsy Amster Literary Enterprises
P.O. Box 277
Los Angeles, CA 90027
213-662-1987; fax: 213-660-4015

David Black Literary Agency
156 Fifth Ave. (Ste. 608)
New York, NY 10010
212-242-5080; fax: 212-924-6609

Barbara Braun Associates Inc.
230 Fifth Ave. (Ste. 909)
New York, NY 10001
212-696-9134; fax: 212-779-4867
email: bba230@earthlink.net

Maria Carvainis Agency Inc.
235 West End Ave.
New York, NY 10023
212-580-1559; fax: 212-877-3486

Julie Castiglia Literary Agency
1155 Camino Del Mar (Ste. 510)
Del Mar, CA 92014
760-753-4361; fax: 760-753-5094

Ruth Cohen Literary Agency
Box 7626
Menlo Park, CA 94025
650-854-2054

The Doe Coover Agency
P.O. Box 668
Winchester, MA 01890
617-721-6000; fax: 617-721-6727

Donadio & Ashworth Inc.
Literary Representatives
121 West 27th St. (Ste. 704)
New York, NY 10001
212-691-8077; fax: 212-633-2837

Candice Fuhrman Literary
Agency
201 Morning Sun Ave.
Mill Valley, CA 94941
415-383-6081; fax: 415-383-9649

Gelfman Schneider Literary
Agents Inc.
250 West 57th St.
New York, NY 10107
212-245-1993; fax: 212-245-8678

Goldfarb & Graybill Law Offices
918 16th St. NW (Ste. 400)
Washington, DC 20006
202-466-3030; fax: 202-293-3187

Sanford J. Greenburger
Associates Inc.
55 Fifth Ave. (15th flr.)
New York, NY 10003
212-206-5600; fax: 212-463-8718

Jellinek and Murray Literary
Agency
109 Nawiliwil St.
Honoloulu, HI 96285
808-395-5972; fax: 808-395-6072

Sarah Lazin Books
126 Fifth Ave. (Ste. 300)
New York, NY 10011
212-989-5757; fax: 212-989-1393

Margaret McBride Literary
Agency Inc.
7744 Fay Ave. (Ste. 201)
La Jolla, CA 92037
619-454-1550; fax: 619-454-2156

Doris S. Michaels Literary
Agency Inc.
One Lincoln Plaza
20 West 64th St. (Ste. 9R)
New York, NY 10023
212-769-2430; fax: 212-873-0774
email: dsmitlag@prodigy.com

The Palmer & Dodge Agency
One Beacon St.
Boston, MA 02108
617-573-0609; fax: 617-227-4420

Jody Rein Books Inc.
7741 S. Ash Court
Littleton, CO 80122
303-694-4430; fax: 303-694-0687
email: jreinbooks@aol.com

Jane Rotrosen Agency
318 East 51st St.
New York, NY 10022
212-593-4330

Bobbe Siegel Literary Agency
41 West 83rd St.
New York, NY 10024
212-877-4985 (voice and fax)

Barbara J. Zitwer Agency
525 West End Ave. (Apt. 7H)
New York, NY 10024
212-501-8423; fax: 212-501-8462

Index

Index